In the Classroom

- Read all of the directions. Make sure you understand them. When you see , be sure to follow the safety rule.

- Listen to your teacher for special safety directions. If you don't understand something, ask for help.

- Wash your hands with soap and water before an activity.

- Wear safety goggles when your teacher tells you to wear them and whenever you see . Wear them when working with anything that can fly into your eyes.

- Wear splash-proof goggles when working with liquids.

- Wear a safety apron if you work with anything messy or anything that might spill.

- If you spill something, wipe it up right away or ask your teacher for help.

- Tell your teacher if something breaks. If glass breaks do not clean it up yourself.

- Keep your hair and clothes away from open flames. Tie back long hair and roll up long sleeves.

- Be careful around a hot plate. Know when it is on and when it is off. Remember that the plate stays hot for a few minutes after you turn it off.

- Keep your hands dry around electrical equipment.

- Don't eat or drink anything during an experiment.

- Put equipment back the way your teacher tells you.

- Dispose of things the way your teacher tells you.

- Clean up your work area, and wash your hands with soap and water.

In the Field

- Always be accompanied by a trusted adult—like your teacher or a parent or guardian.

- Never touch animals or plants without the adult's approval. The animal might bite. The plant might be poison ivy or another dangerous plant.

Responsibility

- Treat living things, the environment, and each other with respect.

McGRAW-HILL
SCIENCE

MACMILLAN/McGRAW-HILL EDITION

RICHARD MOYER ■ **LUCY DANIEL** ■ **JAY HACKETT**

PRENTICE BAPTISTE ■ **PAMELA STRYKER** ■ **JOANNE VASQUEZ**

NATIONAL
GEOGRAPHIC
SOCIETY

McGraw-Hill
School Division

New York   Farmington

PROGRAM AUTHORS

Dr. Lucy H. Daniel
Teacher, Consultant
Rutherford County Schools,
North Carolina

Dr. Jay Hackett
Emeritus Professor of Earth
Sciences
University of Northern
Colorado

Dr. Richard H. Moyer
Professor of Science
Education
University of Michigan-
Dearborn

Dr. H. Prentice Baptiste
Professor of Curriculum and
Instruction
New Mexico State
University

Pamela Stryker, M.Ed.
Elementary Educator and
Science Consultant
Eanes Independent School
District
Austin, Texas

JoAnne Vasquez, M.Ed.
Elementary Science
Education Specialist
Mesa Public Schools,
Arizona
NSTA President 1996–1997

NATIONAL GEOGRAPHIC SOCIETY

Washington, D.C.

CONTRIBUTING AUTHORS

Dr. Thomas Custer
Dr. James Flood
Dr. Diane Lapp
Doug Llewellyn
Dorothy Reid
Dr. Donald M. Silver

CONSULTANTS

Dr. Danny J. Ballard
Dr. Carol Baskin
Dr. Bonnie Buratti
Dr. Suellen Cabe
Dr. Shawn Carlson
Dr. Thomas A. Davies
Dr. Marie DiBerardino
Dr. R. E. Duhrkopf
Dr. Ed Geary
Dr. Susan C. Giarratano-Russell
Dr. Karen Kwitter
Dr. Donna Lloyd-Kolkin
Ericka Lochner, RN
Donna Harrell Lubcker
Dr. Dennis L. Nelson
Dr. Fred S. Sack
Dr. Martin VanDyke
Dr. E. Peter Volpe
Dr. Josephine Davis Wallace
Dr. Joe Yelderman

McGraw-Hill School Division

A Division of The McGraw-Hill Companies

McGraw-Hill School Division
Two Penn Plaza
New York, New York 10121

Printed in the United States of America

ISBN 0-02-277438-6 / 6

4 5 6 7 8 9 027/046 05 04 03 02 01 00

CONTENTS

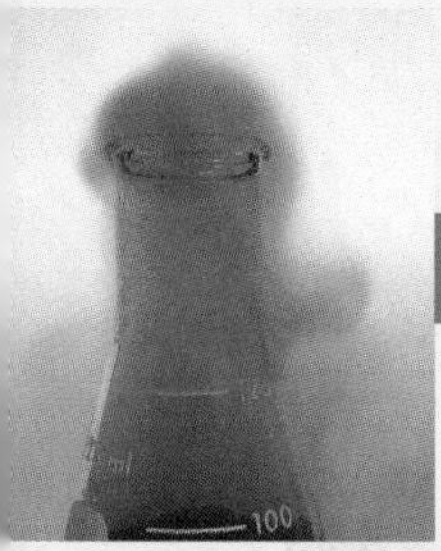

UNIT 1

PROPERTIES OF MATTER AND ENERGY

PHYSICAL SCIENCES

UNIT 2

CELLS, GROWTH, AND REPRODUCTION

LIFE SCIENCES

UNIT 3

FORCES

PHYSICAL SCIENCES

UNIT 4 ASTRONOMY

UNIT 5

THE RESTLESS EARTH

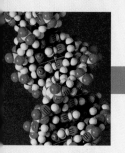

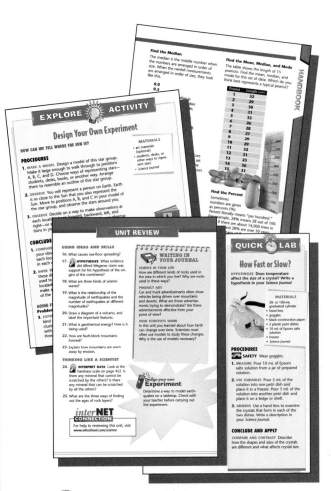

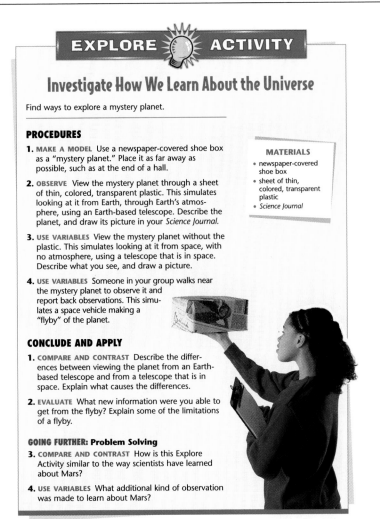

EXPLORE ACTIVITY

Investigate How We Learn About the Universe

Find ways to explore a mystery planet.

PROCEDURES

1. **MAKE A MODEL** Use a newspaper-covered shoe box as a "mystery planet." Place it as far away as possible, such as at the end of a hall.

2. **OBSERVE** View the mystery planet through a sheet of thin, colored, transparent plastic. This simulates looking at it from Earth, through Earth's atmosphere, using an Earth-based telescope. Describe the planet, and draw its picture in your *Science Journal.*

3. **USE VARIABLES** View the mystery planet without the plastic. This simulates looking at it from space, with no atmosphere, using a telescope that is in space. Describe what you see, and draw a picture.

4. **USE VARIABLES** Someone in your group walks near the mystery planet to observe it and report back observations. This simulates a space vehicle making a "flyby" of the planet.

MATERIALS
• newspaper-covered shoe box
• sheet of thin, colored, transparent plastic
• *Science Journal*

CONCLUDE AND APPLY

1. **COMPARE AND CONTRAST** Describe the differences between viewing the planet from an Earth-based telescope and from a telescope that is in space. Explain what causes the differences.

2. **EVALUATE** What new information were you able to get from the flyby? Explain some of the limitations of a flyby.

GOING FURTHER: Problem Solving

3. **COMPARE AND CONTRAST** How is this Explore Activity similar to the way scientists have learned about Mars?

4. **USE VARIABLES** What additional kind of observation was made to learn about Mars?

Design Your Own Experiments, do **Quick Labs**, use **Internet Connections**, and try **Writing in Your Journal**. Use the **Handbook** for help.

Reading Graphs, Diagrams, Maps, and **Charts** help you learn by using what you see.

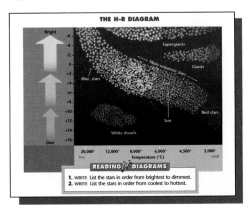

THE H-R DIAGRAM

Bright

Supergiants

Main sequence stars

Giants

Blue stars

Sun

Red stars

White dwarfs

Dim

Temperature (°C)
20,000° 12,000° 8,000° 6,000° 4,500° 3,000°
hot   cool

READING DIAGRAMS
1. **WRITE** List the stars in order from brightest to dimmest.
2. **WRITE** List the stars in order from coolest to hottest.

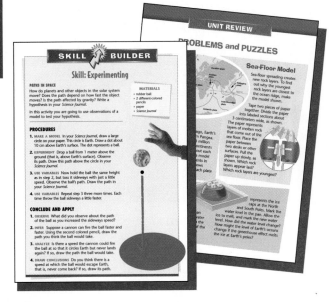

Build your skills with Skill Builders and Problems and Puzzles.

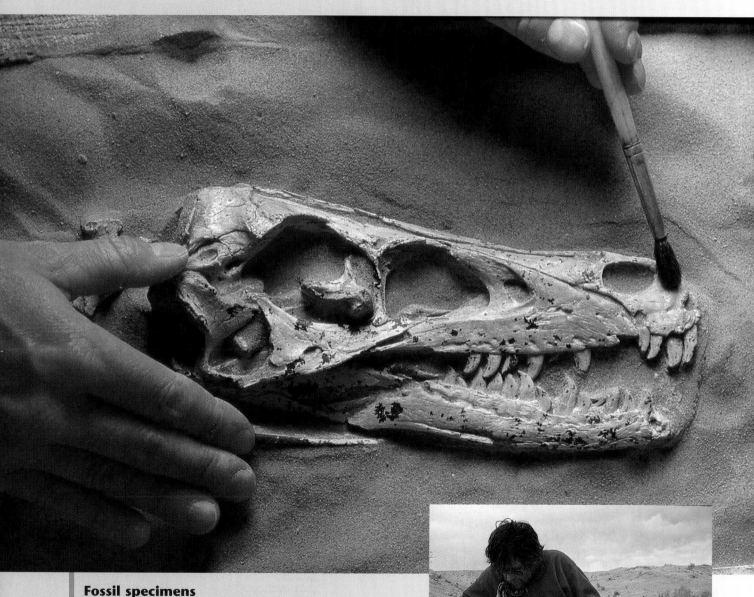

Fossil specimens have to be carefully prepared for shipment.

Novacek and his team have found many dinosaur and mammal fossils.

Michael Novacek

As a boy Michael Novacek was fascinated by a book about the discovery of dinosaur bones in the Gobi, a desert in central Asia. In 1993, as a paleontologist "with a passion for exploring," he made his own discoveries in the Gobi. "We found . . . dinosaur skeletons scattered right on the surface," he says.

As a paleontologist Novacek has traveled all over the world. Every expedition requires long-range planning—started a year in advance— and careful goal-setting. Patience is another requirement. "The hardest thing in the field is when . . . you aren't finding anything," Novacek says. "I often spend nine or ten hours straight just walking around alone, looking for stuff."

Over the years Novacek and his team have discovered a lot of fascinating "stuff," such as a dinosaur embryo in the egg and a parent oviraptor sitting on a nest of eggs. These finds are on display at the Museum of Natural History in New York City, where Novacek works.

In addition to field studies, Novacek spends hours in his research lab. There he enjoys "exploring the links between extinct and living species." One link he has discovered is birds, which he calls "examples of living dinosaurs."

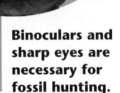

Binoculars and sharp eyes are necessary for fossil hunting.

Relaxing in the field is important, too!

BE A SCIENTIST

SCIENTIFIC METHODS

Have you ever tried the high jump in track? Tried to slam-dunk a basketball? If so, you know how difficult it is to lift yourself very far off the ground. When you jump you are pushing against the powerful pull of Earth. This pull that causes objects to move toward each other is called gravity. Scientists have discovered how gravity works on Earth and in outer space. The information has already helped scientists send space probes to many of the planets in our solar system!

EXPLORE

Does an object's weight affect how it falls? How would you test your idea? Write your answer in your *Science Journal.*

Investigate How Gravity Works

Will a heavy item fall to Earth faster than a lighter item? Can you make items that would normally fall stay in the air without holding them?

Think of a hypothesis about gravity that you can test. A hypothesis is a statement in answer to a question. You must be able to test the statement.

MATERIALS

- large binder clip
- small binder clip
- thin rubber band
- small yogurt container with 2 holes cut opposite each other near the rim
- string
- *Science Journal*

PROCEDURES

SAFETY Always wear goggles when working with rubber bands or when dropping or twirling objects.

1. Attach the small and large binder clips to opposite sides of the rubber band.

2. Hold the smaller binder clip between your fingers, and let the other one hang down. What happens to the rubber band? Why? Write down your ideas in your *Science Journal*.

3. Drop the binder clips and observe them fall. Write down your observations in your *Science Journal*.

4. Repeat the operation several times. Try changing one variable each time you try it again.

5. Now place the binder clips in the yogurt container, and attach the string through the holes on the sides.

6. Move to a place with lots of room around you. Twirl the yogurt container in a big circle so that the yogurt container travels upside down at the top of its arc. Record what happens to the binder clips as they twirl.

CONCLUDE AND APPLY

1. What happened to the rubber band as the clips fell? Why?

2. What happened when you twirled the clips in the container? Did they fall to the ground?

S5

How Does Gravity Work?

The experiments in the Explore Activity are simple to conduct. The difficulty comes in thinking clearly about the results and drawing the right conclusions. Those simple experiments tell us a lot about how gravity works.

When you hold a small binder clip as in the Explore Activity and let the larger one dangle down, you see the rubber band stretch, especially if you add more than one clip. Why? You can think of the rubber band as a kind of spring scale weighing the lower binder clip before you drop it. The heavier the binder clip hanging on the bottom of your spring scale, the farther it will stretch and the lower it will hang.

When the rubber-band scale is dropped, the top clip snaps down and hits the bottom clip. Why? When you let go of the top clip, both the top and bottom clips fall together. This is because, if we ignore air resistance, all objects fall with the same acceleration. If you fell along with the clips, then the clips would seem to float. It is as if there were no gravity. We say that the system is weightless. From the "point of view" of the clips, there is no longer any gravity to oppose the force in the stretched rubber band. This force causes the smaller clip to snap toward the bigger clip.

How can something heavy become weightless? To understand this we need to know more about gravity.

Scientists have shown that gravity is a **force** that can be measured. A force is a push or pull exerted by one object on another.

Before this skydiver's parachute opens, he is in free fall and weightless!

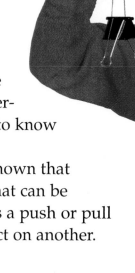

It causes a change in motion. As far as we know, the force of gravity exists among all objects in the universe. That means that any two objects in space, no matter how distant, will attract each other.

Every object has a gravitational pull toward every other object. The force depends on two variables—**mass** (mas) and distance. Mass is the amount of matter in an object. The greater the mass of objects, the stronger their gravitational pull. The closer objects are to one another, the stronger their gravitational pull.

Mass and weight are related but different. An object's mass stays the same. An object's weight can change because it is the force of gravity on it. Astronauts showed how gravity affects weight on the Moon. A 180-pound astronaut weighs only 30 pounds on the Moon! The astronaut can jump six times higher on the Moon, and it takes six times longer to return to the ground!

If we went far enough out into space, far away from other matter, then the force of gravity on us would be weak. We would weigh less, but our mass would stay the same. We would still be made up of the same amount of matter.

WEIGHT OF THE SAME PERSON ON DIFFERENT PLANETS

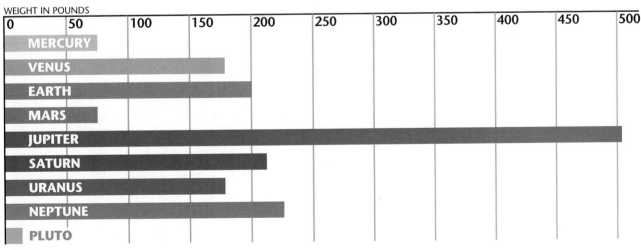

WEIGHT IN POUNDS

0	50	100	150	200	250	300	350	400	450	500

MERCURY
VENUS
EARTH
MARS
JUPITER
SATURN
URANUS
NEPTUNE
PLUTO

How much does the person weigh on each planet?

What Have Scientists Learned About Gravity?

Aristotle was a famous philosopher and scientist who lived more than 2,000 years ago. He said that heavy things fall faster than light things. It seemed like a true statement. Rocks fall to the ground faster than leaves, for instance. He also said that the heavier something is, the faster it will fall. According to his explanation, an object that weighs 10 pounds would fall ten times faster than an object weighing 1 pound.

Aristotle's idea sounded convincing to most people of the day. At that time people were just beginning to question the events around them. They did not have the background that people have today.

Aristotle was wrong. This was shown to be wrong in the Explore Activity. Aristotle could have tried a similar experiment himself, but he didn't.

Not all scientists made the mistake of believing Aristotle. The first to prove Aristotle's theory of weight and gravity wrong was Galileo. In 1589 Galileo conducted his own experiment to see if heavier objects fell faster than lighter ones. Galileo was a science professor at the University of Pisa.

Aristotle's theory on weight and gravity was wrong.

The story is told that one day he climbed to the top of the Leaning Tower of Pisa and dropped a 10-pound weight and a 1-pound weight at the same time. They hit the ground at the same time. A very simple experiment had disproved something that had been believed for centuries.

Other scientists learned from Galileo's discovery. More than 300 years ago, so the story is told, Isaac Newton saw an apple fall from a tree to the ground and thought about it in a whole new way. He thought there might be a connection between the way an apple dropped to the ground and the way the Moon circled Earth instead of flying off into space. Newton was the first to explain and try to measure gravity. His discovery changed our understanding of the universe.

How Do Scientists Get Their Ideas?

Dr. Neil Tyson is an **astrophysicist**. An astrophysicist is a scientist who studies space. *Astro* means "space." A *physicist* studies the properties of matter and energy.

Being a scientist begins with looking around and being curious about the things you see in the world. Dr. Tyson says his whole life changed when he was in sixth grade. One night when he was at a ballgame, a friend passed him a pair of binoculars. He looked at the Moon with them. It was a crescent Moon, and the shadows made it look three-dimensional. He could see the craters and the mountains on the surface.

Dr. Neil Tyson is an astrophysicist.

At that moment he became very curious about the Moon and outer space. He wondered what he could see through a telescope if he could see that much through binoculars!

Being a scientist also means not accepting everything you are told. Even when they are told something, scientists still like to learn about it for themselves. They wonder whether the explanations are as accurate as they could be.

After Dr. Tyson became interested in the Moon, he took a course at the Hayden Planetarium in New York City. A *planetarium* (plan'i târ'ē əm) is a theater with special equipment to show the movements of the Sun, Moon, planets, and stars. The movements are shown by projecting lights on the inside of a dome. Dr. Tyson grew up in a big city where the bright lights prevented him from seeing the stars very well. When he saw the planetarium show, he thought it was fake. He didn't believe all those stars could be out there!

Dr. Tyson decided he would have to find out for himself if the night sky could really look that way. When he grew up, he became a scientist. He has observed space through many of the world's most powerful telescopes. In fact he is now the director of the Hayden Planetarium!

How Do Scientists Work?

Being a scientist means comparing things and trying to find explanations for how things work. It often means making small models that can explain big things or making models on Earth that can explain things in outer space.

This was shown in the Explore Activity. When the string was pulled, the container and the clips in it started to move. All objects tend to oppose changes in their motion. This is known as **inertia** (i nûr′shə). To change the motion, a force is needed. The greater the mass of an object, the greater the force needed. The inertia of the container and clips would have kept them moving in a straight line. However, the string pulled inward on the container, keeping it on a circular path. The container, in turn, pulled inward on the clips, keeping them on a circular path. An inward force toward the center of a circle is called a **centripetal** (sen trip′i təl) **force**.

When the container was at the top of its path, there were two forces acting down on the clips. These forces were gravity and the force of the container pushing down on the clips. Why, then, didn't the clips fall out of the container? The reason is that the clips were moving sideways at a very fast speed. This made them both fall and move sideways at the same time. The result was the circular path you observed.

The Explore Activity can help you understand how the Moon orbits around Earth. The Moon is moving very fast. Its inertia would send it flying off into space if not for the pull of gravity. The combination of the Moon's inertia and the pull of gravity between Earth and the Moon keeps the Moon circling Earth. In the same way, you kept the yogurt container and clips moving in a circle.

This combination of inertia and gravity is also what keeps a **satellite** (sat'ə lit') orbiting Earth. A satellite is any object that revolves around another object. The Moon is a satellite of Earth. However, satellites like the space shuttle need to travel very fast to maintain the balance. The shuttle needs to travel at 28,000 kilometers per hour (18,000 miles per hour) to stay in orbit around Earth.

Scientists are curious about the world around them. This curiosity causes them to ask questions about things they don't understand. Sometimes they question the explanations accepted by others. As recently as 100 years ago, scientists believed that the idea of galaxies outside our own was untrue. Strong telescopes have shown scientists evidence of millions of more galaxies!

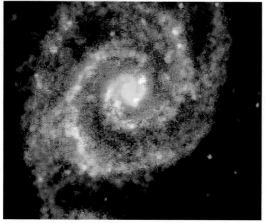

Milky Way galaxy

Dr. Tyson studies how galaxies form and change. He is especially interested in our own Milky Way galaxy. The problem with studying it is we cannot easily see its structure because we are inside of it. That is why Dr. Tyson studies distant galaxies. He uses them as models of our own galaxy to search for clues they might offer to explain our own galaxy.

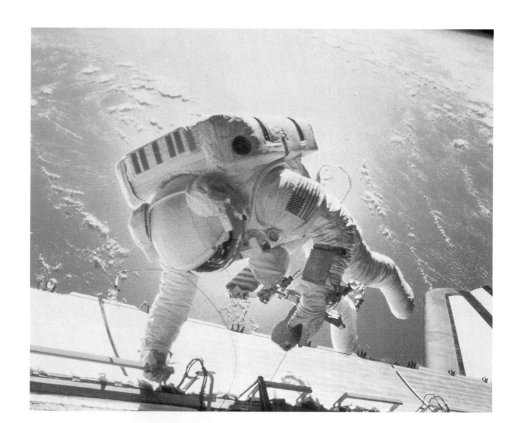

An astronaut in space

How Can I Be Like a Scientist?

Science starts with questions about the things around us. Why doesn't the Moon fly off into space? How can people travel upside down on a roller coaster and not fall to the ground? Do things have weight when they are falling? Why do I feel strange going down fast in an elevator? You may have observed things around you that made you wonder about questions like these. Being a scientist means trying to find answers to questions like these. It means not believing the wrong or incomplete explanations of others.

Scientists conduct experiments to test their ideas. To understand things that are too far away to measure, they think of ways to compare them with things we know more about. For example, to understand things about outer space, they often try to study the way things work here on Earth.

Now let's go back and look at how ideas about gravity, weight, and mass were tested in the Explore Activity.

You Asked Yourself Questions

To start an experiment, you asked some questions. Will a heavy item fall to Earth faster than a lighter item? Can I make items that would normally fall stay in the air without holding them? How can I test my ideas to learn more about how gravity works?

You Set Up an Investigation

The sentence you wrote at the beginning of the Explore Activity was a **hypothesis**. Remember, a hypothesis is a statement that can be tested by observation. You planned an experiment to test your hypothesis. You weighed the objects on the scale and observed what happened when you dropped them. You recorded and organized the information to help you understand it.

An important part of an experiment is changing one part of it to affect the outcome. The factor changed in an experiment to affect the outcome is a **variable**. In the Explore Activity, one variable that could be changed was the height from which the binder clips were dropped.

identify or learn about an object or event

plan think out ahead of time how something is to be done or made, including methods and materials

predict state possible results of an event or experiment

reproduce results repeat an experiment to verify the findings

revise examine and improve

sequence a series of things that are related in some way

test the examination of a substance or event to see what it is or why it happens

theory an explanation based on observation and reasoning

use numbers ordering, counting, adding, subtracting, multiplying, and dividing to explain data

These are new Science Words that you learned in Be a Scientist. You will see and learn more Science Words printed in blue as you read this book.

astrophysicist a scientist who studies how things work in space

centripetal force the force on an object in motion away from a central point

force a push or pull exerted by one object on another, causing a change in motion

gravity a force of attraction that exists between any objects with mass

hypothesis a statement that can be tested by observations

inertia the tendency of an object to oppose a change in motion

mass the amount of matter in an object

satellite any object that revolves around another object

variable something in an experiment that can be changed or controlled

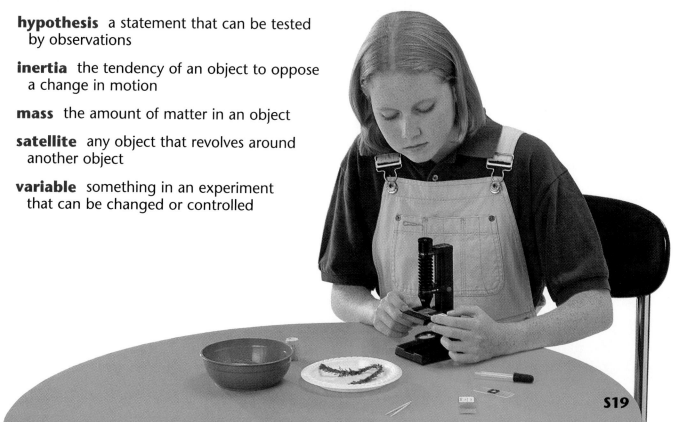

METHODS OF SCIENCE

Here is a chart that shows the steps to follow when solving a problem in science.

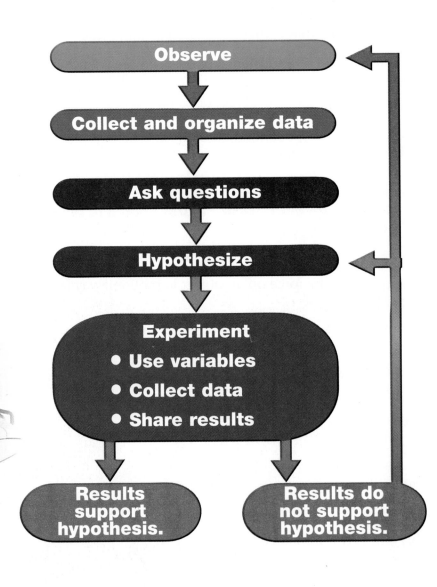

Observe

Collect and organize data

Ask questions

Hypothesize

Experiment
- Use variables
- Collect data
- Share results

Results support hypothesis.

Results do not support hypothesis.

READING CHARTS

WRITE How would you solve a problem in science? Write a paragraph based on the chart.

PROPERTIES OF MATTER AND ENERGY

CHAPTER 1

PROPERTIES AND CHANGES

Did you know that both of the objects shown are made out of the same substance? However, one sparkles, while the other is dark. How could they be made out of the same substance?

In this chapter learn how substances can change and still stay the same—and how they change into new substances.

 In this chapter summarize what you read. That is, sum up in a sentence or two what you read before you turn to a new page.

WHY IT MATTERS

Find out how taking a deep breath helps you float in water.

SCIENCE WORDS

matter any solid, liquid, or gas

mass amount of matter in an object

volume the amount of space an object takes up

density the amount of mass in a certain volume of material

physical property a property that can be observed without changing the identity of a substance

physical change a change in size, shape, or state without forming a new substance

solution a mixture of one substance dissolved in another so that the properties are the same throughout

chemical change a change in matter that produces a new substance with different properties from the original

Physical Properties

What happens when large quantities of oil spill into ocean water? How does this problem affect living things in the ocean?

Luckily oil spills can be cleaned up. Can you tell why? Oil floats on top of the water. It does not sink down into the water. It can be cleaned off the surface of the water.

Why does oil float on water? Does the weight of oil and of water have anything to do with it?

EXPLORE

HYPOTHESIZE How can the fact that a substance floats help you identify the substance? Why does one substance float over another? Write a hypothesis in your *Science Journal*. Test your ideas.

Science, Technology, and Society

Look around. Nearly everything you see is some kind of mixture. When you look at the clouds, you're seeing ice suspended in air! Seawater, soil, air, and most rocks and metals are mixtures too.

Solutions If you add spoonful after spoonful of white salt to a glass of water and stir it, the salt disappears. Or does it? Taste the solution and you'll know the salt's still there!

Colloidal Suspensions Colloids contain small particles. How small? Put sand in water, and it sinks. Grind that sand into colloid-size particles, mix them with water, and the sand seems to disappear.

Other Suspensions A solid can be suspended in a liquid if its particles are big enough for gravity to make them rise or fall. For example, cream rises to the top of milk. Homogenizing milk turns fat particles to colloids.

Mixing Metals About 5,000 years ago, people began mixing solids by first making them liquid. They dissolved tin in copper. When the two liquid metals cooled, they produced bronze, a metal far stronger and harder than pure copper! This heavy metal launched a new age in human history. Later people mixed carbon and iron and launched the Iron Age.

Information Age Mixtures You're living in a new age that was launched with the invention of the computer chip. Computer chips are made by mixing solid substances, such as boron or arsenic, into pure silicon.

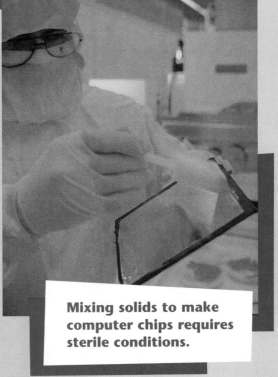

Mixing solids to make computer chips requires sterile conditions.

Discussion
Starter

1 If you mix ordinary table salt and table sugar, how can you tell which is which without tasting?

2 Describe the following mixtures: smoke, paint, gasoline, brass, soda water, blood.

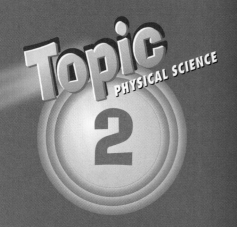

WHY IT MATTERS

You use many different substances every day.

SCIENCE WORDS

element a substance that cannot be broken down any further into anything simpler

atom the smallest particle of an element that has the same chemical properties as the element

nucleus an atom's dense center, where most of its mass is

electron a negatively charged particle that moves around an atom's nucleus

proton a positively charged particle inside an atom's nucleus

neutron a particle with no charge inside an atom's nucleus

atomic number the number of protons in an atom

metal any of a group of elements that conduct heat and electricity, is shiny and bendable

Elements and Atoms

What holds this building together? If you could look to see what kinds of pieces, or units, are within the walls, what would you see? How do you know?

What is inside a diamond? A glass of water? A balloon filled with helium gas? What do you think are the units that make up diamond, water, and helium?

EXPLORE

HYPOTHESIZE What if you were given a mystery box with things inside? How could you tell what was inside the box without looking inside it? Write a hypothesis in your *Science Journal.* Test your ideas.

How Have Ideas About Atoms Changed?

In 1803 John Dalton proposed that atoms were solid, like tiny marbles that had no particles inside. By 1898 experiments by J. J. Thomson showed that atoms contained electrons. Thomson proposed that the electrons in atoms were sprinkled throughout a positive fluid, like raisins in a pudding.

By 1913 Ernest Rutherford and H. G. J. Moseley showed that the positive matter in atoms was packed into a tiny nucleus. The electrons were thought to orbit the nucleus. However, since 1926 scientists have thought of electrons as "clouds" surrounding the nucleus. They are not like planets traveling around the Sun.

The atoms of each element have a unique number of protons. This number is called the element's **atomic number**. Carbon atoms, for example, have 6 protons, while sodium atoms have 11 protons. The number of protons in an atom tells us what element it is.

Any element's atoms can occur in different forms. The atoms of an element have the same number of protons but may have different numbers of neutrons. The mass of any atom is sometimes thought of as the total number of protons and neutrons. The electrons have so little mass, they hardly contribute to the total. Since the atoms of an element may come in different forms, we can state an average atomic mass for each element.

VIEWS OF ATOMS OVER THE PAST 200 YEARS

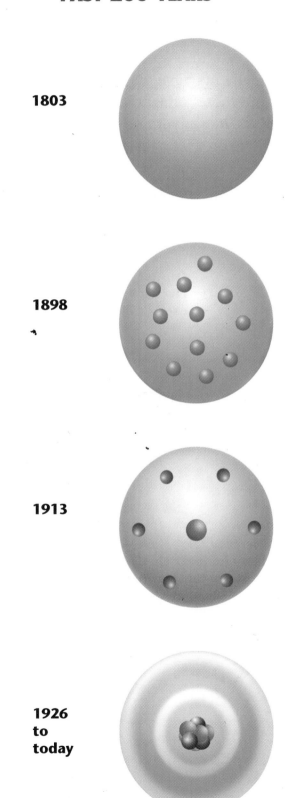

1803

1898

1913

1926 to today

What Are Elements Like?

Scientists have discovered over 100 different elements, but only about 50 of them are commonly found on Earth. That means that only 50 elements combine to form all the substances you see and use every day.

Elements have all sorts of different properties. Some are hard, shiny solids, like silver and aluminum. Others are clear gases that you can't see or taste, like oxygen and helium. Still others are liquids.

These photographs illustrate different elements. Notice that each square includes the element's atomic symbol.

2 He Helium

Helium (He) is a lightweight gas. It makes balloons rise through the air.

Copper (Cu) conducts electricity very well, so it is used in electrical wiring.

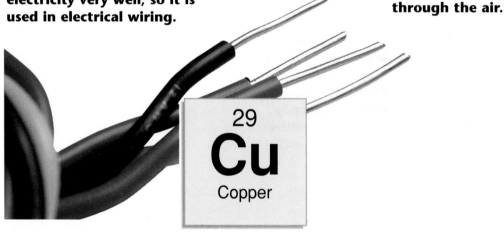

29 Cu Copper

Mercury (Hg) is one of the few elements that is a liquid at room temperature.

80 Hg Mercury

Sulfur (S) is a yellow powder in its element form. Compounds made of sulfur often smell very bad— like rotten eggs.

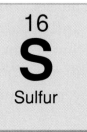

16 S Sulfur

18
Al
Aluminum

Aluminum (Al) is light and strong. Aluminum is used for lots of products, including airplane parts and soft-drink cans.

HEALTH LINK

Calcium (Ca) is never found as an element in nature. But compounds that contain calcium are very common. Milk is a good source of calcium, which your body needs for healthy bones and teeth.

20
Ca
Calcium

QUICK LAB

Element Lineup

HYPOTHESIZE Some elements are more alike than others. How can you tell which are most alike? Different? Write a hypothesis in your *Science Journal.*

MATERIALS
- element samples (iron, copper, carbon, aluminum)
- sandpaper
- hand lens
- *Science Journal*

PROCEDURES

1. **PLAN** All the samples but one belong to a main group of similar elements. Can you tell which belong? Which does not? Decide how you will start. Write your ideas in your *Science Journal.*

2. **OBSERVE** Use the hand lens to look closely at each sample. Note any differences in your *Science Journal.*

3. **OBSERVE** Rub each sample with sandpaper. What can you learn about each?

CONCLUDE AND APPLY

1. **ANALYZE** Which characteristics help you identify the most similar samples?

2. **ANALYZE** Which sample is most different from the others? How can you tell?

Are There Patterns in the Properties of Elements?

By the 1800s scientists had noticed that many elements had very similar properties. Did these similarities have any meaning? Could there be a pattern to the elements?

In 1868 a Russian scientist named Dmitry Mendeleyev was experimenting with arranging the elements in different ways. When he arranged them according to atomic mass, he discovered a repetitive pattern to several properties, including density, metal character, and ability to react with other elements. Any repeating pattern is called periodic. Mendeleyev's discovery is called the periodic table of elements.

Mendeleyev's periodic table proved to be very successful. One reason was because he left blank spaces in the table when necessary to keep the periodic pattern. To explain the blank spaces, Mendeleyev boldly predicted that elements would be discovered to fill them! Sure enough, scientists soon discovered three elements—scandium, gallium, and germanium. Each had just the right properties to fill a blank space in Mendeleyev's table.

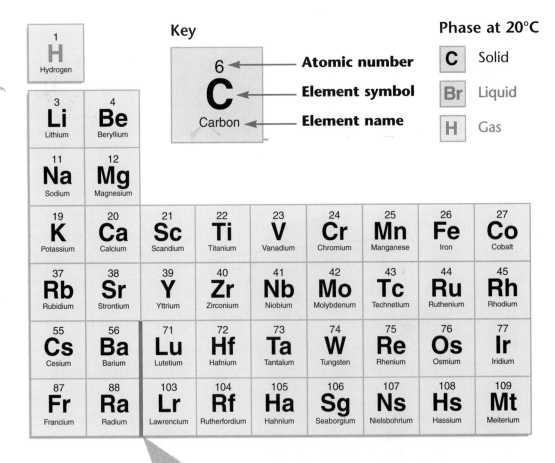

What Is the Modern Periodic Table Like?

In Mendeleyev's day, only 60 elements were known. Today at least 112 elements are known, some of them artificial. The modern form of the periodic table is shown below. The elements are arranged in order of increasing atomic number. The vertical columns contain elements that react with other substances in similar ways. They are chemically alike.

Each row of elements in the table is called a period. Notice that the periods become wider and wider as you move down the table. The first period has only 2 elements—hydrogen and helium. The sixth and seventh periods, on the other hand, have 32 elements each.

According to their properties, elements can be placed in one of three groups—**metals**, *metalloids* (met′ə loidz′), and *nonmetals*. Metals conduct heat and electricity, are shiny when polished, and bend rather than break. Nonmetals are just the opposite. Metalloids have only some properties of metals.

Metallic Properties

Li	Metal
B	Metalloid
C	Nonmetal

								2 **He** Helium
			5 **B** Boron	6 **C** Carbon	7 **N** Nitrogen	8 **O** Oxygen	9 **F** Fluorine	10 **Ne** Neon
			13 **Al** Aluminum	14 **Si** Silicon	15 **P** Phosphorus	16 **S** Sulfur	17 **Cl** Chlorine	18 **Ar** Argon
28 **Ni** Nickel	29 **Cu** Copper	30 **Zn** Zinc	31 **Ga** Gallium	32 **Ge** Germanium	33 **As** Arsenic	34 **Se** Selenium	35 **Br** Bromine	36 **Kr** Krypton
46 **Pd** Palladium	47 **Ag** Silver	48 **Cd** Cadmium	49 **In** Indium	50 **Sn** Tin	51 **Sb** Antimony	52 **Te** Tellurium	53 **I** Iodine	54 **Xe** Xenon
78 **Pt** Platinum	79 **Au** Gold	80 **Hg** Mercury	81 **Ti** Thallium	82 **Pb** Lead	83 **Bi** Bismuth	84 **Po** Polonium	85 **At** Astatine	86 **Rn** Radon
110	111	112						

63 **Eu** Europium	64 **Gd** Gadolinium	65 **Tb** Terbium	66 **Dy** Dysprosium	67 **Ho** Holmium	68 **Er** Erbium	69 **Tm** Thulium	70 **Yb** Yttebium
95 **Am** Americium	96 **Cm** Curium	97 **Bk** Berkelium	98 **Cf** Californium	99 **Es** Einsteinium	100 **Fm** Fermium	101 **Md** Mendelevium	102 **No** Nobelium

What Are Metals and Nonmetals?

About three-fourths of the elements are metals. As a group metals conduct electricity. The metal copper is generally used for electric wires. The wires inside a cord for a lamp or a stereo set are made of copper. To be safe, a rubber coating covers the wires in electrical appliances. Substances such as rubber and plastic are not good conductors of electricity.

A thin wire made of the metal aluminum would melt if electricity passed through it. Aluminum is not a good choice for wires. However, aluminum and copper both are used for many pots and pans because they conduct heat.

Sodium metal is so reactive that it has to be stored in oil.

To make silver more durable in jewelry and silverware, it is mixed with other metals.

Chlorine, a nonmetal, is very reactive and poisonous.

This beautiful diamond is made of pure carbon, a nonmetal. Diamonds are one of the hardest substances known.

Some metals also change chemically when exposed to air or water. Iron rusts when it combines with the oxygen in air or with dissolved oxygen in water. You can see rusting happen along bicycle and car fenders.

Nonmetals tend to have the properties opposite to metals. Most nonmetals are poor conductors of heat and electricity. One nonmetal, bromine, is a liquid at room temperature. The others are all gases or solids at room temperature. The solid nonmetals are brittle rather than bendable. They can't be stretched into a thin wire as copper can.

What Are Metalloids?

On the periodic table, the elements boron, silicon, germanium, arsenic, antimony, tellurium, polonium, and astatine lie on the borderline between metals and nonmetals. These elements are known as the metalloids. Their properties fall in between the properties of metals and nonmetals. An important use of metalloids is to make materials that conduct electricity in useful ways.

Silicon is the most abundant element in Earth's solid surface. Sand is made of silicon dioxide, a chemical combination of silicon and oxygen.

In this piece of computer circuitry, the peach-colored material is mostly silicon. The dark paths are silicon combined with boron or arsenic. The circuit works because the dark paths conduct electricity better than the surrounding silicon.

WHY IT MATTERS

You use metals in many ways every day. Copper wires conduct electricity in the walls of houses and schools. A thin metal wire in an incandescent light bulb gets hot enough to glow when electric current goes through it.

You also use metallic mixtures, called alloys. Steel is a mixture of iron and a nonmetal, carbon. Steel is used to make cars, bridges, and even paper clips.

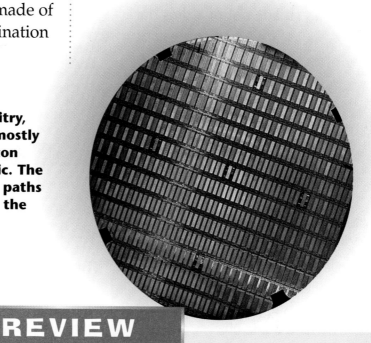

REVIEW

1. What do you think atoms are?

2. When electricity is passed through water, the water breaks down into two simpler gases. Could water be an element? Why or why not?

3. Why did scientists have to rely on indirect evidence to discover how atoms are put together?

4. **USE NUMBERS** The atomic number of chlorine is 17. What does this tell you about chlorine atoms?

5. **CRITICAL THINKING** *Analyze* Of sulfur, argon, and sodium, which has chemical properties like oxygen? Why?

WHY IT MATTERS THINK ABOUT IT
How do you use metals at home? At school? For sports? Why are metals used for many objects?

WHY IT MATTERS WRITE ABOUT IT
How might using metals be a problem for the environment?

Atoms Through Time

Aristotle, another Greek, teaches that the world is made not of atoms but of four elements—earth, air, water, and fire. He's usually right, so no one questions his idea for nearly 2,000 years!

Robert Boyle, an English scientist, separates and combines substances. He reports that elements can't be broken down and that compounds are combinations of elements. More than 100 years later, French chemist Antoine Lavoisier proves Boyle's theory.

| 465 B.C | 384 B.C. | 1661 | 1803 |

Democritus, a philosopher in ancient Greece, suggests that matter is made of atoms, but he can't prove it. *Atom* is Greek for "unbreakable."

The English chemist John Dalton proves that atoms exist. He determines a compound's elements, then calculates the weight of each element's atom in that compound. He discovers that atoms of different elements have different weights. However, he thinks a compound has only one atom of an element, so water is HO. Italian scientist Amadeo Avogadro discovers that a compound can have more than one atom of an element, as in H_2O.

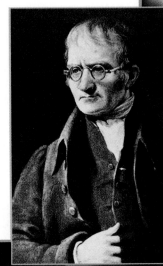

Ancient Greece
(dark brown)

Mediterranean Sea

A Closer Look

Litmus paper turns red if it touches an acid and blue if it touches a base.

DISCUSSION STARTER

1. Where on the pH scale would you find a substance with many more H+ ions than OH– ions?

2. Is tasting a good way to find out if a substance is an acid or a base? Why or why not?

To learn more about acids and bases, visit *www.mhschool.com/science* and select the keyword LITMUS.

*inter***NET**
CONNECTION

SCIENCE WORDS

chemical
   change p.12

density p.5

electron p.22

endothermic p.44

exothermic p.44

ion p.37

matter p.4

neutron p.22

physical
   change p.8

proton p.22

volume p.4

USING SCIENCE WORDS

Number a paper from 1 to 10. Fill in 1 to 5 with words from the list above.

1. The amount of space an object takes up is called its ___?___.

2. A positively charged particle in the nucleus of an atom is called a(n) ___?___.

3. A(n) ___?___ reaction releases heat.

4. A neutral particle in the nucleus of an atom is called a(n) ___?___.

5. Boiling and freezing are examples of ___?___.

6–10. Pick five words from the list above that were not used in 1 to 5, and use each in a sentence.

UNDERSTANDING SCIENCE IDEAS

11. Describe two ways that atoms can combine to form a compound.

12. What is the difference between mass and density?

13. Describe how the periodic table is arranged.

14. Explain the difference between metals and nonmetals.

15. Explain the difference between a physical and a chemical change.

USING IDEAS AND SKILLS

16. If you seal an empty glass pickle jar and drop it in water it floats. How can it float if the glass is denser than water?

17. **READING SKILL: SUMMARIZE** A friend doesn't believe atoms exist. What evidence might convince your friend atoms do exist?

18. Why would it be improper to speak of an NaCl molecule?

19. **USE NUMBERS/COMMUNICATE** A compound called sulfuric acid (H_2SO_4) can form from the combination of sulfur dioxide and water. Could one molecule of sulfur dioxide (SO_2) combine with one molecule of water (H_2O) to form sulfuric acid? Explain.

20. **THINKING LIKE A SCIENTIST** You shaped a lump of clay into a tiny dog. Describe a method you could use to find the volume of the clay.

PROBLEMS and PUZZLES

Egg Float Put an egg in a glass of water. Does it float? What happens if you add salt to the water? Why?

CHAPTER 2
TEMPERATURE, HEAT, AND ENERGY

What are these objects? Is it a coincidence that they are facing the Sun? Have you ever seen anything like them on a house or a building?

In this chapter learn about energy—what it is, how we get it and use it, and what the Sun has to do with it.

 In this chapter pay attention to the order, or sequence, of steps or events that you read about.

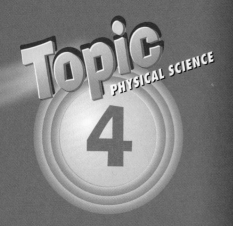

WHY IT MATTERS

Microwave ovens heat foods with a special kind of radiation.

SCIENCE WORDS

kinetic energy the energy of a moving object

potential energy energy stored in an object or material

temperature the average kinetic energy of the molecules in a material

heat energy that flows between objects that have different temperatures

radiation the transfer of energy by electromagnetic waves

conduction the transfer of energy by direct contact of molecules

convection the transfer of energy by the flow of a liquid or gas

insulation prevents heat from flowing in or out of a material

Temperature and Heat

What kinds of things can you feel with your skin? Your skin is filled with nerve endings. They are sensitive to touch, to pressure, to pain, and to hot and cold.

How good is your skin at telling hot from cold? Usually it is good enough to trigger you to pull your hand away from extreme heat or cold—even before you get a chance to think about it. Why is that important?

EXPL🔘RE

HYPOTHESIZE Is your skin a good tool for measuring warm and cool? Can anything affect the way your skin senses warmth? Write a hypothesis in your *Science Journal*. How might you test it safely?

Earth Science Link

Since 1850 the average temperature on Earth has risen 1°C (1.8°F). Some scientists predict it will rise 2°C (3.5°F) more by the year 2100. They believe this will lead to many problems, including the melting of polar ice caps that would cause sea levels to rise and flood coastal areas.

At the troposphere's outer edge, temperatures are –51°C to –79°C (–60°F to –110°F). The ozone layer traps the Sun's radiation, so temperatures rise. In the thermosphere it may be 1,200°C (2,200°F)!

DISCUSSION STARTER

1. What is global warming?

2. How have people contributed to an increase in Earth's temperatures?

Exosphere

Thermosphere

Mesosphere

Stratosphere

Troposphere

To learn more about global warming, visit *www.mhschool.com/science* and select the keyword TEMPS.

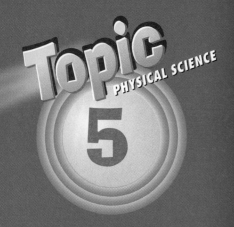

Topic 5
PHYSICAL SCIENCE

WHY IT MATTERS

Ice cools a warm drink by absorbing heat.

SCIENCE WORDS

thermal expansion the expansion of matter when its temperature is raised

pressure the force on each unit of area of a surface

melting the change of a solid into a liquid

vaporization the change of a liquid to a gas as molecules break free from each other

condensation the change of a gas into a liquid as molecules attract each other

freezing the change of a liquid into a solid

boiling the formation of bubbles of vapor that escape from a liquid that is being heated

evaporation the vaporization of molecules from the surface of a liquid

Temperature, Heat, and Matter

What effect does heating have on the air? These balloonists use burners to heat the air in each balloon's bag. Why does a balloon filled with heated air rise?

EXPLORE

HYPOTHESIZE How does heat affect a gas? How might it affect matter in general? Write a hypothesis in your *Science Journal*. Test your ideas.

Investigate What Heat Can Do to Matter

See how the size of a balloon is affected by hot and cold.

MATERIALS
- 2 identical balloons
- pan of warm water
- pan of ice water
- modeling compound or clay (optional)
- *Science Journal*

PROCEDURES

1. Blow up the balloons so that both are the same size. Tie each balloon so that no air escapes.

2. USE VARIABLES Put one balloon aside, away from either pan of water.

3. EXPERIMENT Put the second balloon into the warm water for five minutes.

4. COMPARE Remove the balloon from the water. Compare its size with the size of the first. Record your observations in your *Science Journal*.

5. EXPERIMENT Place the second balloon in the ice water for five minutes. Repeat step 4.

CONCLUDE AND APPLY

1. EXPLAIN Why did you put the first balloon aside?

2. COMMUNICATE What happened when you put the balloon in warm water? In ice water?

3. DRAW CONCLUSIONS How does heat affect a gas?

GOING FURTHER: Problem Solving

4. HYPOTHESIZE How might your results change if you used two equal cubes of modeling compound or clay instead of the balloons? How would one cube compare to the other if one was heated in warm water? Cooled in ice water? Write a hypothesis. Test your ideas.

What Can Heat Do to Matter?

What happens to a gas that is heated? The Explore Activity showed that a gas expands when it is heated. In general any kind of matter expands when its temperature is raised. We call this effect **thermal expansion**.

For example, as the coolant in a car becomes hotter, it expands. The plastic container shown in the photograph provides extra space for hot coolant to expand into. When the engine is cool, the fluid contracts and no longer overflows into the container.

A bimetallic strip is made of two different metals fused together. When heated one metal expands more than the other. This causes the strip to bend. Bimetallic strips are used in thermostat switches that turn devices on or off depending on temperature.

If it were not for separations placed between sections of the walkway, like those shown in the photograph, the walkway might buckle and bend on the hottest days. Similar separations are placed in concrete sidewalks and roadways to prevent damage due to thermal expansion.

The steel in this roadway expands on hot days and contracts on cold days.

Cars have a liquid coolant that flows through the engine to remove excess heat.

A bimetallic strip

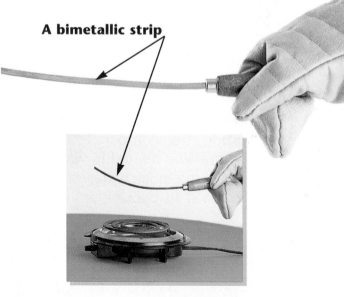

History of Science

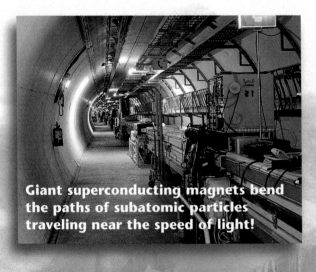

Giant superconducting magnets bend the paths of subatomic particles traveling near the speed of light!

It was later discovered that lead or mercury frozen at about 4 K became superconductors. Superconducting magnets, much more powerful than others, are vital in "atom smashers."

DISCUSSION STARTER

1. What three different ways of cooling are mentioned here?

2. Suggest some possible applications of superconductivity. Discuss why these have or have not occurred.

Large rockets use liquid oxygen, nicknamed LOX.

To learn more about the really cold, visit *www.mhschool.com/science* and select the keyword CRYOGENIC.

*inter*NET
CONNECTION

Topic 6
PHYSICAL SCIENCE

WHY IT MATTERS

Fossil fuels will not last forever. We should use them wisely.

SCIENCE WORDS

solar cell a device that generates an electric current from sunlight

biomass conversion getting energy from plant and animal materials by changing them into high-quality fuels

nuclear fission the splitting of a nucleus with a large mass into two nuclei with smaller masses

chain reaction a reaction that is kept going by products of the reaction

nuclear fusion the merging of nuclei with smaller masses into a nucleus with a larger mass

hydroelectricity the use of flowing water to generate electricity

thermal pollution the excess heating of the environment

Sources of Energy

How many kinds of energy do you use each day? How much energy do you use? How might you tell?

Where does all the energy you use each day come from? One way or another, most of our energy supplies come from sunlight. How is this home using sunlight directly as a source of heat?

EXPLORE

HYPOTHESIZE How can you use the Sun's energy for useful purposes, such as to cook food? Write a hypothesis in your *Science Journal*. Test your ideas.

SCIENCE WORDS

boiling p.71

condensation p.71

conduction p.57

evaporation p.71

freezing p.71

heat p.55

hydroelectricity p.89

kinetic energy p.53

melting p.70

potential
  energy p.53

pressure p.68

solar cell p.81

USING SCIENCE WORDS

Number a paper from 1 to 10. Fill in 1 to 5 with words from the list above.

1. A(n) __?__ captures sunlight to make electricity.

2. Electricity from falling water is called __?__.

3. The process of changing from liquid to solid is called __?__.

4. Molecules colliding against a container create __?__.

5. The energy of motion is called __?__.

6–10. **Pick five words from the list above that were not used in 1 to 5, and use each in a sentence.**

UNDERSTANDING SCIENCE IDEAS

11. How does energy change when a roller coaster slides down a track?

12. What are three methods of transferring heat?

13. What are two types of nuclear reactions?

14. Describe the various ways matter can change its state.

15. What is the source of most of Earth's energy?

USING IDEAS AND SKILLS

16. What if you put a pan on a table? Would you expect heat to travel from the pan to the table, making the pan colder and the table hotter. Why?

17. **READING SKILL: SEQUENCE OF EVENTS** Describe the changes a sample of steam (gaseous water) would undergo as heat is steadily removed from it.

18. Consider a piece of nuclear fuel that contains nuclei that can be split by neutrons. As the size of the piece becomes smaller, it is less likely that a chain reaction can be maintained. Suggest a reason why.

19. **USE VARIABLES** What if you have samples of 6 different fabrics? Design an experiment to show which fabric best keeps an object warm. In your experiment identify the variable you are testing and the variables you are controlling.

20. **THINKING LIKE A SCIENTIST** Imagine that you want to build a solar-heated home. Describe all the characteristics the ideal location for a solar home would have.

PROBLEMS and PUZZLES

Glass Act Some window panes are coated with a dark material that absorbs sunlight. Why is this done? Do you think this is a good thing to do in all climates?

UNIT 1 REVIEW

SCIENCE WORDS

chain reaction p.84   metal p.27

chemical bond p.35   molecule p.38

compound p.34   potential

conduction p.57   energy p.53

convection p.57   pressure p.68

density p.5   proton p.22

exothermic p.44   thermal

hydroelectricity   expansion p.66

p.89

USING SCIENCE WORDS

Number a paper from 1 to 10. Beside each number write the word or words that best complete the sentence.

1. The quantity of matter in a unit of volume is a measure of the __?__ of the matter.

2. A positively charged particle in the nucleus of an atom is a(n) __?__.

3. An element that conducts electricity efficiently, is shiny, and bends easily is called a(n) __?__.

4. A chemical reaction that gives off heat is __?__.

5. Atoms are held together in molecules by __?__.

6. If you mix hot and cold water, all of the water becomes the same temperature due to __?__.

7. The extreme sag of a power line on a hot, sunny day is an example of __?__.

8. The quantity of force on a unit of area is a measure of the __?__ on a surface.

9. A process that continues by itself is called a(n) __?__.

10. A rotating water turbine at a dam produces __?__.

UNDERSTANDING SCIENCE IDEAS

Write 11 to 15. For each number write the letter for the best answer. You may wish to use the hints provided.

11. Which is a chemical change?
    a. iron melting
    b. iron rusting
    c. iron bending
    d. iron filed into powder
    (Hint: Read page 12.)

12. The number of protons in an atom is its
    a. mass
    b. atomic weight
    c. atomic number
    d. charge
    (Hint: Read page 23.)

13. Which of the following is a chemical reaction?
    a. condensation
    b. evaporation
    c. synthesis
    d. convection
    (Hint: Read page 40.)

14. What causes thermal expansion?
    a. chemical change
    b. increased motion of molecules
    c. change in gas pressure
    d. reduction of volume
    (Hint: Read page 67.)

15. Solar cells generate electricity from
    a. light
    b. water
    c. chemical changes in batteries
    d. pressure
    (Hint: Read page 81.)

USING IDEAS AND SKILLS

16. What is a change of state of matter? How are these changes made?

17. Explain why Mendeleyev's table is useful.

18. Why is copper used for electrical wire?

19. How does a compound differ from a mixture?

20. 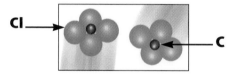 **USE NUMBERS/COMMUNICATE** Give the formula for this compound. How do you know what subscript number to use with Cl?

Cl ——→ ←—— C

21. Why is it better to use a thermometer to determine the temperature of things instead of using touch?

22. How do we get heat from the Sun?

23. Which methods of producing electricity require chemical reactions?

THINKING LIKE A SCIENTIST

24.  **USE VARIABLES** Review the experiment on page 59. Explain how to control the variables time and amount of heat.

25. Explain why a bimetallic strip bends when it is heated.

interNET CONNECTION

For help in reviewing this unit, visit
www.mhschool.com/science

WRITING IN YOUR JOURNAL

SCIENCE IN YOUR LIFE

List things that you use that have electric motors. Tell how these things make work easy for you. What would your life be like without them?

PRODUCT ADS

Describe the types of housing insulation used in your part of the country. Is it more important to keep heat in or out? Why is that so? What resources can insulation save?

HOW SCIENTISTS WORK

Drawing diagrams of a process helps scientists to understand it. Make your own diagram that shows how hydroelectricity is a form of solar energy. See page 89.

Design your own Experiment

What if you have two rods that are the same size and shape but made of different metals? Make a hypothesis about how to find out which is the better conductor of heat. Design an experiment to test your hypothesis. Review your experiment with your teacher before you attempt it.

PROBLEMS and PUZZLES

Ancient Elements

Until the late 1700s, people believed that there were only four elements—earth, air, fire, and water.

What if you could return to the 18th century in a time machine? How could you convince people that earth, air, fire, and water were not elements? Fill out a chart like the one shown.

	Why It's Not an Element	How You Could Prove It
Earth		
Air		
Fire		
Water		

Coolereeno Coolers

Coolereeno Coolers come in two different varieties—clear Morning Slush and dark purple Midnight Blue. When left in sunlight, Morning Slush stays cool. Midnight Blue gets warm. Can you think of a reason for why this happens?

Try an experiment to show the effect on Coolereeno Coolers. Put two clear bottles in sunlight—one with water in it, the other with inked water in it. Cap both bottles, and measure their temperatures after an hour. Which one stays cooler?

The Tire Mystery

In the cool morning, Tina's bike tires had only 50 pounds of pressure in them. In the hot afternoon, Tina rode to the gas station and put 60 pounds of pressure into her tires. The next morning it was cool. Tina checked her tires and found they had 50 pounds of pressure again.

She repeated the process. She filled her tires, but the following morning her tires were low again. Finally, Tina brought her bike to the bike shop. The bike mechanic told Tina there was nothing wrong with her tires. Can you explain what was causing them to drop in pressure on cool mornings?

UNIT 2

CELLS, GROWTH, AND REPRODUCTION

CHAPTER 3

CELLS

Have you ever wondered what happens inside a plant to make it grow?

You are growing, too—and will keep growing until you are an adult. What makes people grow?

To understand how living things grow, you might start by asking what living things are made of.

In this chapter you will compare and contrast many things. To *compare* means to tell how things are alike. To *contrast* means to tell how things are different.

WHY IT MATTERS

Living things play an important role in their surroundings.

SCIENCE WORDS

cell the basic unit of life

tissue a group of similar cells working together at the same job

organ a group of different tissues working together to do certain jobs

organ system different organs working together to do certain jobs

organism any living thing that can carry out its life activities on its own

population all the organisms of the same kind living in the same place

community all the populations living together in the same place

ecosystem the living and nonliving things in an area interacting with each other

Organization in Living Things

How can you tell a living thing from a nonliving thing? What do all living things have? What do they all do?

Do all living things move, for example? Compare a jet and a plant. If the jet moves and the plant does not, does that mean that the jet is a living thing and the plant is not? Are there traits that all living things share?

EXPLORE

HYPOTHESIZE Can you tell whether something is or was alive by looking at it under a microscope? Is there some special characteristic that allows you to tell? Write a hypothesis in your *Science Journal*. Test your ideas.

Design Your Own Experiment

WHAT ARE LIVING THINGS MADE OF?

PROCEDURES

1. OBSERVE Look at samples under a microscope. For example, try placing a few grains of salt on a microscope. Do not add a coverslip. Observe it under low power. Draw what you see in your *Science Journal.*

2. COLLECT DATA Design your own data table for recording the details of what you observe.

3. EXPERIMENT You might try repeating step 1 with sand.

4. OBSERVE Repeat under low power, and draw what you see. Select your own samples. Use such samples as a wet-mount slide of a small piece of tomato skin, an *Elodea* leaf, a drop of yeast on a clean microscope slide with a coverslip over it, a prepared slide of human blood, and a wet-mount slide of a thin piece of cork.

MATERIALS

- microscope
- 4 microscope slides
- microscope coverslip
- dropper
- water
- toothpick
- few grains of salt
- few grains of sand
- tomato skin
- *Elodea* leaf
- yeast
- prepared slide of human blood
- thin piece of cork
- *Science Journal*

CONCLUDE AND APPLY

1. OBSERVE Describe the appearance of each of the specimens you observed.

2. CLASSIFY Classify the specimens you observed into two groups.

3. INTERPRET DATA What is the greatest difference between these two groups?

GOING FURTHER: Problem Solving

4. CLASSIFY What other specimens do you think would fit into your two groups? Explain.

5. ASK QUESTIONS What are some other things you might fit into these two groups?

What Do All Living Things Do?

Why do all living things need food? Because they need raw materials and energy to live and grow. They need the right temperatures in their surroundings. They meet their needs by carrying out certain activities.

When you eat you take in raw materials and energy needed to live and grow.

ACTIVITIES OF LIVING THINGS

- **NUTRITION** This is the intake and use of food by living things. All living things need food. Food provides the raw materials and energy for growth, repair, and other activities of living things.

- **RESPIRATION** After food is digested, it combines with oxygen, and energy is released. Respiration is the process by which energy is released from food. This process produces wastes. When you exhale you give off two waste products—water and carbon dioxide.

- **EXCRETION** Wastes from respiration and other activities can build up in your body. Some wastes are poisons. Fortunately living things can perform a special activity to remove such materials. The removal of wastes produced by living things is called excretion.

- **RESPONSE AND MOVEMENT** Living things respond, or react, to changes in their surroundings. For example, when you are cold, your body responds by shivering, which helps to warm you. Another type of response is movement. If you are outside and it starts to rain, you run inside. Plants also respond to their surroundings by moving. They slowly bend toward the sunlight.

- **GROWTH** All living things grow. To grow means to either increase in size or increase in the amount of material contained.

- **REPRODUCTION** The process by which living things produce offspring is called reproduction. Reproduction allows each kind of living thing to exist on Earth for a long period of time.

READING N CHARTS

1. **DISCUSS** Of the activities listed, is there any activity that nonliving things also do?
2. **WRITE** Is there any activity that nonliving things never do?
3. **REPRESENT** Organize your answers to numbers 1 and 2 into a list.

What Are Living Things Made Of?

Are living things made of elements just as nonliving things are? Living things are made of elements such as carbon, hydrogen, and oxygen. In addition, living things are organized into units or parts that make up the living things. The Explore Activity showed what some of these parts are.

The life activities listed on page 100 are carried out in the smallest part of a living thing. This basic unit of life is called a **cell**. All living things are made up of cells. Some living things are made up of only one cell. As you might guess, you'd need a microscope to see them. Many-celled living things, such as complex plants and animals, are made up of different kinds of cells, each with its own special function.

Plants and animals have cells that to a great extent have the same parts. However, there are important differences between them. Plant cells have a stiff outer covering, whereas animal cells do not. This covering helps a plant to stand upright. Many plant cells also contain a green substance that traps the energy of sunlight and enables the cells to produce their own food.

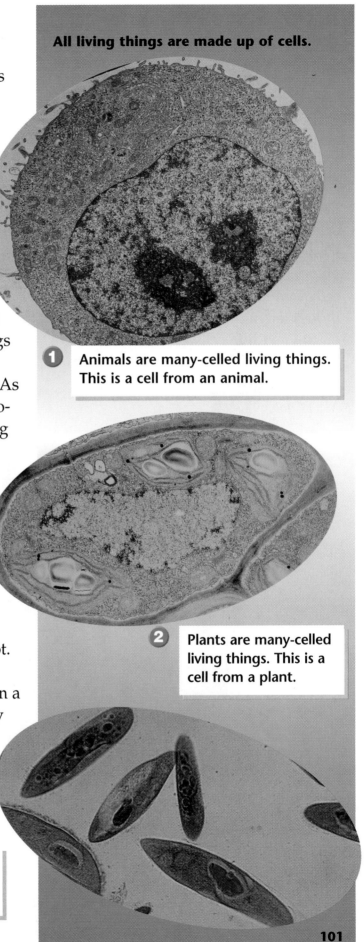

All living things are made up of cells.

1 Animals are many-celled living things. This is a cell from an animal.

2 Plants are many-celled living things. This is a cell from a plant.

3 Bacteria, paramecia, and euglena carry out all of life's functions in a single cell.

What Types of Cells Were Discovered First?

Who was the first person to see cells? The first cells were seen in 1665 by Robert Hooke, an English scientist. He looked at cork under a microscope and saw little "boxes" that looked like the "cells" of a honeycomb. The invention of the microscope in the early 17th century enabled scientists such as Hooke to begin their exploration of the microscopic world. Although the cork cells that Hooke observed were not living, techniques were developed later on to view live cells.

Since Hooke's first observation of cells, improved microscopes have allowed us to make cells appear to be hundreds or thousands of times their actual size. This allows us to examine and study the cells. It was not until the work of Anton van Leeuwenhoek (lā'vən hük'), beginning in 1673, that a new world of one-celled living things was opened up. Leeuwenhoek was the first to observe one-celled living things such as bacteria and paramecia.

Brain Power

What would you need to make a microscope? What parts would you need? What forms of energy? How would you make it work?

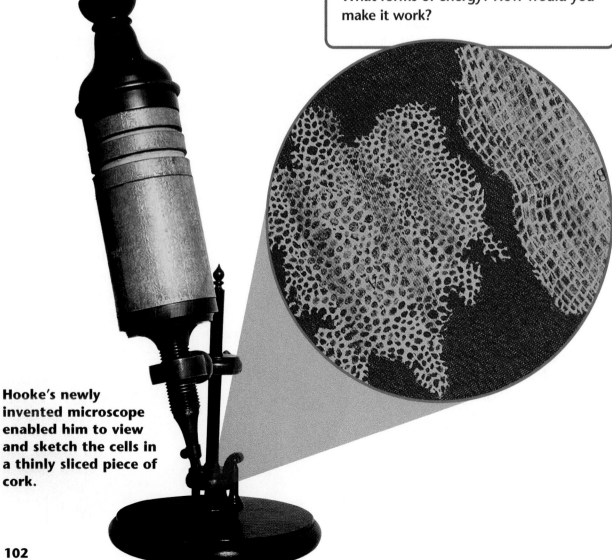

Hooke's newly invented microscope enabled him to view and sketch the cells in a thinly sliced piece of cork.

No two kinds of animals in the picture meet their needs in exactly the same way.

What Is the Function of Living Things in a Community?

Many populations can live in the same area because each kind of living thing has a certain function in the community. For example, one function of a barn cat in a farm community is to eat mice and other rodents.

What a living thing eats, when it eats, and where it eats are also part of its function. The way a living thing reproduces and raises its young is also part of its function.

You've learned that organisms interact with each other in communi-

ties. But how do they interact with nonliving things in their environment? Nonliving things include soil, water, and air. Fish depend on water for getting oxygen and for moving. Air carries pollen from one plant to another so that seeds can be made.

These relationships form an **ecosystem**. An ecosystem is made up of the living and nonliving things in an area interacting with each other.

107

How Do Organisms Interact with Nonliving Things?

A rotting tree stump is a small ecosystem. Cities, redwood forests, polar regions, and oceans are examples of larger ecosystems. How would you describe your ecosystem?

Food Chains

In every ecosystem there is a feeding relationship between the organisms. When animals eat plants, the energy of plants is passed to the animals. These animals are then eaten by other animals. These animals, in turn, may be eaten. Each time, food energy passes from one living thing to the next.

Some organisms get their food by breaking down dead organisms into nutrients. The energy is passed from the dead organism to the organism breaking it down.

Each organism is like a link in a *food chain*. A food chain is a model of how the energy in food is passed from organism to organism in an ecosystem.

A rotting tree stump is a small ecosystem. Here insects, bacteria, and other organisms all interact with one another.

Bracket fungi and moss may grow on the cool, dark side of the trunk.

Leaf litter—leaves, twigs, and bark—provides food and shelter for slugs, snails, beetles, and flies.

Who Lives Where?

Can a water lily grow in a desert? Why or why not? The nonliving parts of an ecosystem, such as water, temperature, and soil, determine what can live there. An organism must have certain characteristics in order to survive in any given ecosystem. A water lily, for example, could not survive in the desert. On the other hand, a cactus can survive in the desert because its thick covering keeps it from drying out.

The interaction between nonliving and living parts causes changes in the ecosystem. In time, as conditions change, one or more populations may be replaced by other populations.

Living things are organized internally from cells to tissues to organs to organ systems. They are also organized into populations and communities, based on the way they get along or interact in their environment. Some populations provide food for others. Many plants, for example, provide food.

The lichens on a rock shown below are the beginning of a series of changes leading to a spruce-fir forest.

REVIEW

1. **COMPARE AND CONTRAST** How are living and nonliving things alike? How are they different?

2. Why do cells in a many-celled organism differ?

3. How are living things put together?

4. Give some examples of a population.

5. **CRITICAL THINKING** *Analyze* What if divers find a rocklike object on the sea floor. How would they decide if it is a living thing?

WHY IT MATTERS THINK ABOUT IT
How do you interact with the other kinds of living things in your area?

WHY IT MATTERS WRITE ABOUT IT
What populations provide you with food? Do these populations live in your area? If not, how have people managed to solve the problem?

READING SKILL
Pick two cells that you learned about in this lesson. Write a description that compares and contrasts them.

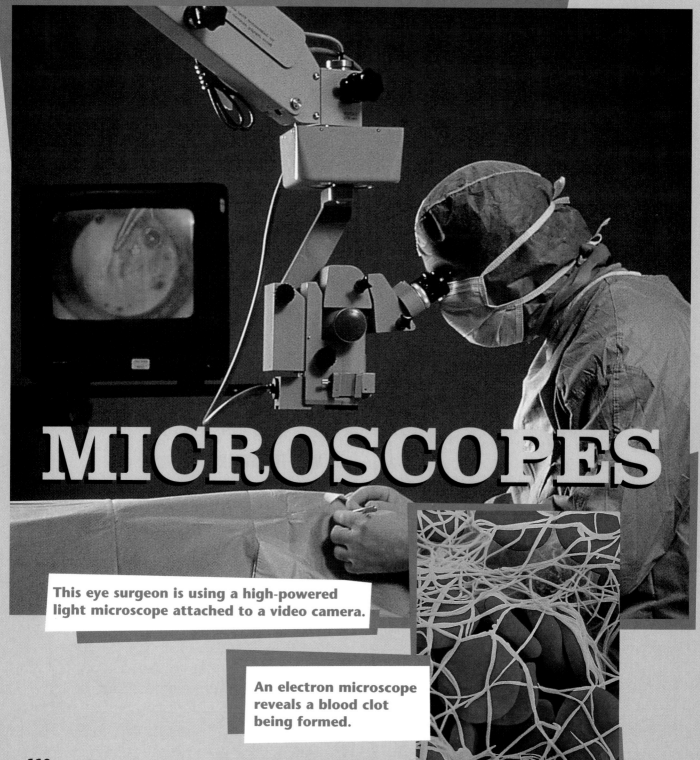

MICROSCOPES

This eye surgeon is using a high-powered light microscope attached to a video camera.

An electron microscope reveals a blood clot being formed.

Seeing things too small to be seen by the naked eye became possible for the first time during the Middle Ages, when glass makers created single-lens microscopes. Around 1590 Dutch glass makers arranged two lenses in a tube to make the first compound microscope. In 1665 English scientist Robert Hooke used a compound microscope to discover cells.

In 1677 Anton van Leeuwenhoek in Holland, using a microscope he invented, discovered bacteria and other one-celled organisms. During the 1800s improved microscopes made possible Louis Pasteur's discoveries of microbes and the relationship between bacteria and disease.

In 1933 Ernst Ruska invented a microscope powerful enough to reveal tiny viruses and parts of cells. It used electron beams rather than light waves. Today's scanning electron microscopes make dramatic three-dimensional images. Scanning tunneling microscopes can map the contours of atoms. The same technology allows scientists to move atoms and to build molecules.

These silicon atoms were mapped by a scanning tunneling microscope.

Discussion
Starter

In what ways might the ability to move single atoms be useful?

inter
CONNECTION To learn more about microscopes, visit
www.mhschool.com/science and enter the keyword **SCOPE.**

Topic
LIFE SCIENCE
2

WHY IT MATTERS

Knowing about cells can help you plan meals.

SCIENCE WORDS

cell membrane a cell's outer covering

nucleus the densest part of a cell, which controls a cell's activities

chromosome a strand in the nucleus that stores directions for cell activities

cytoplasm a gel-like substance inside the cell membrane, where most cell activities occur

mitochondrion a rod-shaped structure that supplies the cell with energy

vacuole a sac-like storage space in a cell

cell wall a stiff covering outside the cell membrane of a plant cell

chloroplast a green structure in a plant cell where food is produced

A Closer Look at Cells

What makes a water lily different from a parrot? Are they alike?

You might say they are different because one is a plant and the other an animal. What makes all plants and animals different?

How are they alike? One thing they have in common is that all plants and animals are made up of cells. Do you think they have the same kinds of cells? Explain.

EXPLORE

HYPOTHESIZE How might the cells of plants and animals be different? Would you be able to recognize each if you saw them? Write a hypothesis in your *Science Journal*. Test your ideas.

EXPLORE ACTIVITY

Investigate What Is Inside Cells

Look through a microscope to find out what is inside cells.

PROCEDURES

1. OBSERVE Make a wet-mount slide of a leaf from the tip of an *Elodea* plant. Use the dropper to place a drop of water on the slide. Holding the leaf tip with forceps, drop it onto the water that is on the slide. Holding the cover slip by the edges, lower it onto the top of the leaf. Observe the leaf on low power, focusing on the top layer of cells. Focus on one cell. Describe what you see in your *Science Journal.*

2. COMMUNICATE Look at the center of a cell on high power. Draw the *Elodea* cell, labeling the different structures that you can see. Return the microscope to low power. Remove and clean the slide and coverslip.

3. COMPARE Get a prepared slide of cheek cells from your teacher. Locate the cells on low power. Repeat step 2.

CONCLUDE AND APPLY

1. COMPARE Describe the similarities and differences in your observations of the *Elodea* cell and the human cheek cell.

GOING FURTHER: Apply

2. EXPERIMENT Do other cells look more like an *Elodea* cell or a human cheek cell? Make a wet mount of a thin onion skin to test your ideas.

MATERIALS

- microscope
- microscope slide
- coverslip
- forceps
- dropper
- *Elodea* plant leaf
- prepared slide of human cheek cells
- onion skin (optional)
- *Science Journal*

Human cheek cells

Elodea plant

Elodea cells

What Is Inside Cells?

The Explore Activity showed that cells have smaller parts inside. Do you think all cells have the same kinds of parts? Animals have many different kinds of cells in their bodies. What parts do these different kinds of animal cells have in common? The answer to this question is shown in the diagram. The earliest microscopes showed the outer edge of a cell clearly.

Cell Parts

As microscopes improved, they showed that cells have small parts. Each part has a special function.

- All cells have an outer covering, called a **cell membrane**, that gives the cell shape and helps control materials that move in and out of the cell.

- The largest, most visible part of the cell, the **nucleus** (nü′klē əs) (plural, *nuclei*), is separated from the cytoplasm by its own membrane. The nucleus is the control center of the cell. It directs the cell's activities.

- Long strands called **chromosomes** (krō′mə sōmz′) can be found in the nucleus. They are like blueprints of the cell. They store directions for cell activities. They transfer the directions to the next generation of cells.

CELL PARTS

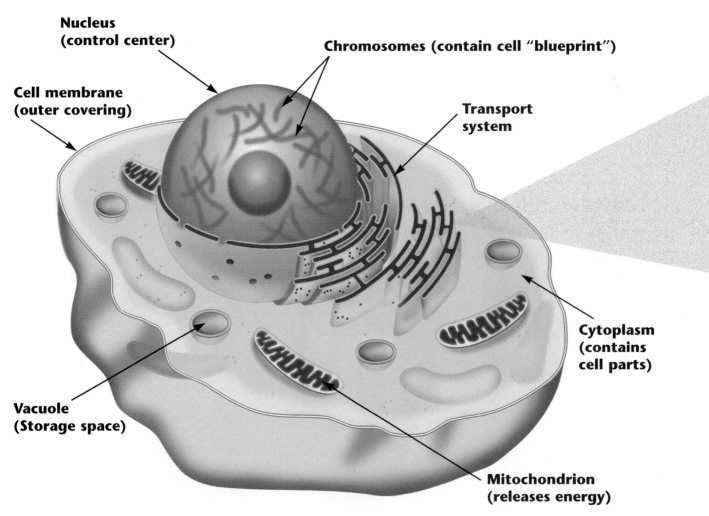

Nucleus (control center)

Chromosomes (contain cell "blueprint")

Cell membrane (outer covering)

Transport system

Cytoplasm (contains cell parts)

Vacuole (Storage space)

Mitochondrion (releases energy)

- **Cytoplasm** (sī′tə plaz′əm), the gel-like substance inside the cell membrane, contains a large amount of water. Most of the cell's life processes take place within the cytoplasm. It also contains chemicals and other cell structures that carry out special jobs for the cell. Scientists found that different structures within the cytoplasm have different functions.

- Rod-shaped structures, called **mitochondria** (mī′tə kon′drē ə) (singular, *mitochondrion*), are often referred to as the "powerhouses" of the cell. They package and secrete materials containing energy, which can be used by the cell.

As researchers learn and understand more about the structure and function of the cell, we gain more knowledge about how these tiny factories work together in the complex organ systems of plants and animals.

- **Vacuoles** (vak′ū ōlz′) are sac-like storage spaces in cells. They store anything, from wastes (prior to removal) to food.

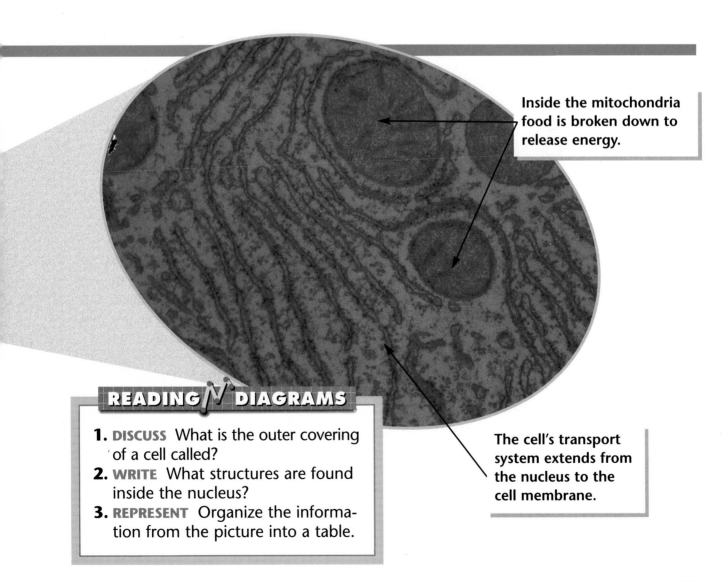

Inside the mitochondria food is broken down to release energy.

The cell's transport system extends from the nucleus to the cell membrane.

READING IN DIAGRAMS

1. **DISCUSS** What is the outer covering of a cell called?
2. **WRITE** What structures are found inside the nucleus?
3. **REPRESENT** Organize the information from the picture into a table.

What Is Inside Plant Cells?

The Explore Activity referred to both plant and animal cells. Both cells had several structures in common. What are these structures?

If you were to compare a lion with a rosebush, you would find many differences. When the individual cells of these organisms are compared, they have many characteristics in common. Cells are the basic units of structure and function for both plant and animal cells. Many of these cells have the same types of structures.

Look at this picture of a cell from the leaf of a green plant. What things do you find that are also in animal cells?

PLANT CELL

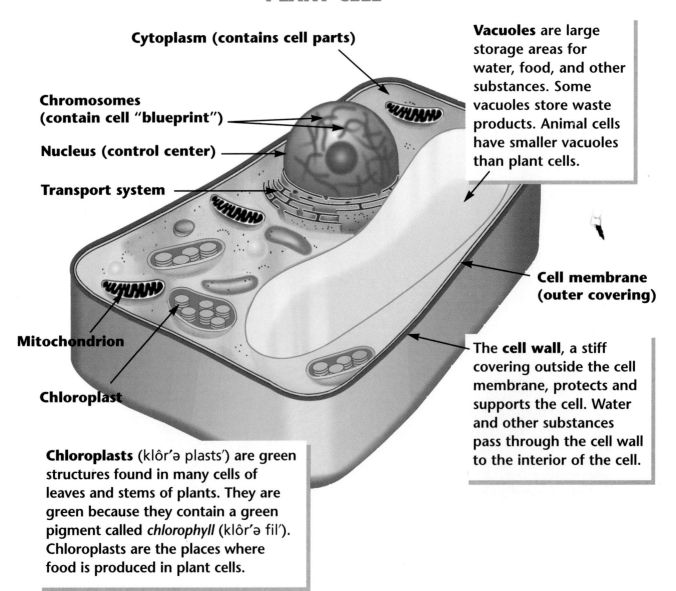

Cytoplasm (contains cell parts)

Chromosomes (contain cell "blueprint")

Nucleus (control center)

Transport system

Mitochondrion

Chloroplast

Vacuoles are large storage areas for water, food, and other substances. Some vacuoles store waste products. Animal cells have smaller vacuoles than plant cells.

Cell membrane (outer covering)

The **cell wall**, a stiff covering outside the cell membrane, protects and supports the cell. Water and other substances pass through the cell wall to the interior of the cell.

Chloroplasts (klôr′ə plasts′) are green structures found in many cells of leaves and stems of plants. They are green because they contain a green pigment called *chlorophyll* (klôr′ə fil′). Chloroplasts are the places where food is produced in plant cells.

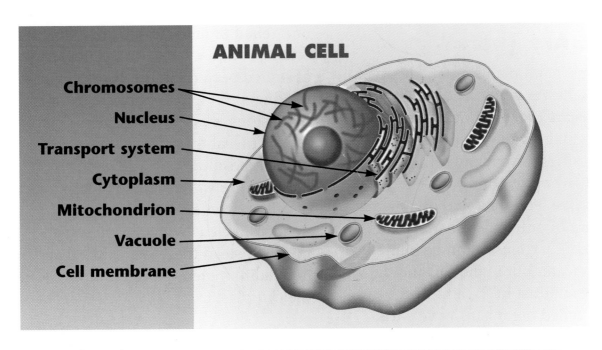

ANIMAL CELL

- Chromosomes
- Nucleus
- Transport system
- Cytoplasm
- Mitochondrion
- Vacuole
- Cell membrane

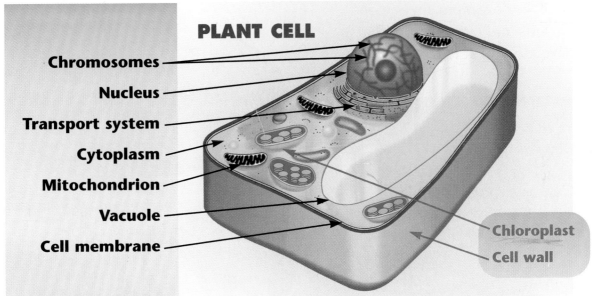

PLANT CELL

- Chromosomes
- Nucleus
- Transport system
- Cytoplasm
- Mitochondrion
- Vacuole
- Cell membrane
- Chloroplast
- Cell wall

How Do Plant Cells and Animal Cells Compare?

Plant cells contain some structures that are not found in animal cells. Compare the diagram of the typical plant cell with that of the animal cell. Which cell structures are found only in plant cells? Why do you think that plant cells have these structures and animal cells do not?

READING DIAGRAMS

1. **DISCUSS** Which of the parts shown here are also in animal cells?
2. **WRITE** What parts that are in both plant and animal cells look different in size?
3. **REPRESENT** Make a table to show how animal cells and plant cells are different.

What Other Kinds of Cells Are There?

Animals and plants are made up of many cells. As you learned in Topic 1, the cells are organized into tissues, organs, and organ systems. Do all living things have many cells? If you look at a drop of pond water under a microscope, you may find organisms made up of only one cell. Many kinds of *one-celled organisms* can be found not only in water but in the soil and on particles of dust in the air.

One-celled organisms have parts that you can find in cells of animals and plants. For example, an amoeba has a nucleus and cytoplasm. What other parts do you see?

Bacteria (singular, *bacterium*) are one-celled organisms, too. The Dutch scientist Anton van Leeuwenhoek first observed bacteria in the 1670s when looking at scrapings from his teeth and the insides of animals. Modern microscopes reveal that bacteria have a cell membrane and a cell wall, something like plant cells. But unlike other kinds of cells, bacteria do not have a clearly defined nucleus with chromosomes inside. Instead these cells have their hereditary material located throughout the cytoplasm.

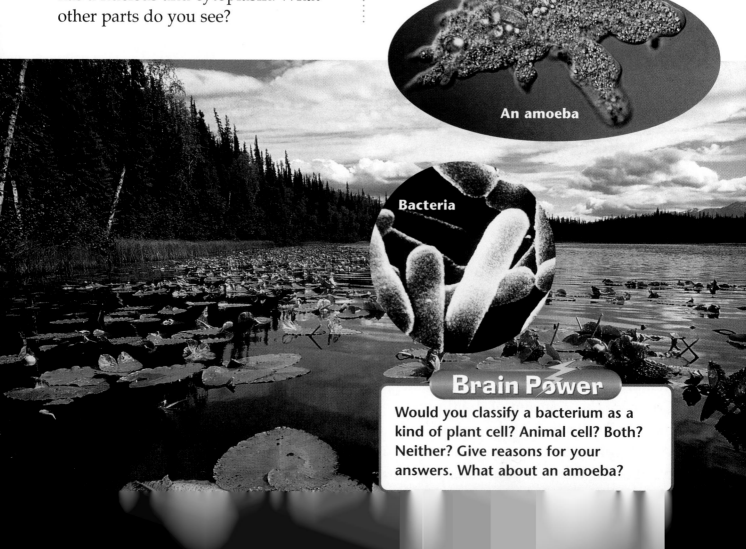

An amoeba

Bacteria

Brain Power

Would you classify a bacterium as a kind of plant cell? Animal cell? Both? Neither? Give reasons for your answers. What about an amoeba?

History of Science

Scientists develop ways of staining and fixing tissues to preserve cells in a lifelike state.

German scientist Rudolf Virchow discovers that cells divide to form new cells. Scientists had thought cells formed from air or nothing!

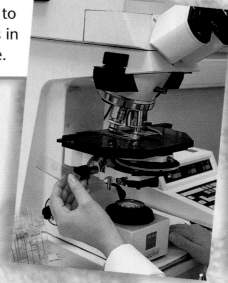

We know the cell theory:
- All living things are made of one or more cells.
- Cells are the basic units of living things.
- All cells come from other cells.

| 1858 | 1860s–1890s | 1940s | Today |

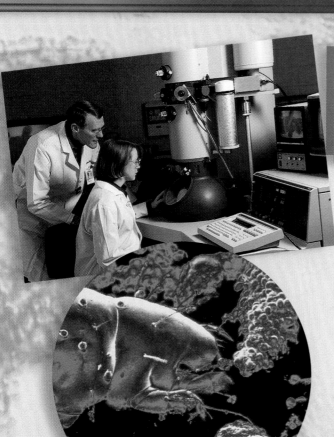

Electron microscopes, 200 times more powerful than light microscopes, help scientists better understand what happens in cells.

DISCUSSION STARTER

1. Why did scientists think that cells formed from air or nothing?

2. Why did it take so long from the discovery of cells to knowing they are part of all living things?

To learn more about cells, visit **www.mhschool.com/science** and select the keyword CORK.

*inter*NET
CONNECTION

Topic 3
LIFE SCIENCE

WHY IT MATTERS

Cell activities can help people survive.

SCIENCE WORDS

diffusion the movement of molecules from higher to lower concentration

osmosis the diffusion of water through a cell membrane

active transport the movement of molecules through a cell membrane, requiring energy

photosynthesis the food-making process in producers using sunlight

respiration the release of energy from sugar molecules

fermentation a form of respiration without oxygen

How Cells Work

Is this diver in any danger from the shark that looms outside the cage? Could smaller fish get into the cage?

How can a cage and diver be compared to a cell? The diver is surrounded by a cage. A cell is surrounded by a cell membrane. What might the cell membrane let in or keep out of a cell?

EXPLORE

HYPOTHESIZE Does the size of a particle affect what can pass through a membrane? Write a hypothesis in your *Science Journal*. Test your ideas.

Investigate What Can Pass Through a Barrier

Use a tea bag to explore what can go through a membrane.

PROCEDURES

SAFETY Be careful with scissors.

1. Fill a jar with warm water. Place the tea bag in the water, and add 1 tsp. of sand.

2. **OBSERVE** Shake the jar, then leave it undisturbed for 15 minutes. Record your observations. Be sure to look for the sand.

3. **COMPARE** Remove the tea bag from the jar, and place it on the paper towel. Cut the tea bag open with scissors. Record what you observe in your *Science Journal*.

MATERIALS

- small jar with a lid
- tea bag
- warm water
- 1 tsp. of sand
- clock or timer
- scissors
- paper towel
- plastic teaspoon
- *Science Journal*

CONCLUDE AND APPLY

1. **OBSERVE** What color was the water in the container after 15 minutes? Was the color evenly distributed?

2. **DRAW CONCLUSIONS** What entered the tea bag? What moved out of the tea bag?

3. **INFER** What do you think determines which particles move into or out of a tea bag?

GOING FURTHER: Problem Solving

4. **EXPERIMENT** What if you used food coloring instead of sand? What color of food coloring would you use to see the results?

127

How Can Things Move In and Out of a Cell?

Substances are flowing in and out of cells through the cell membrane all the time. Cells use substances to grow and get energy. How does it work? The clue is that cells are in a moist environment. The process works something like ink and water.

What would happen if you placed a drop of food coloring in a bowl of water? You would probably observe the water slowly turn color. Molecules of substances are in constant motion, even though you may not see the motion. As they move about, they often collide and bounce off one another.

This movement causes the food-coloring molecules to spread farther apart until they are evenly spaced throughout the water. This process, called **diffusion**, occurs when molecules of a substance move from an area of higher concentration to an area of lower concentration. That is, the molecules move from where they are crowded to where they are less crowded.

Diffusion also occurs in gases. If you open a bottle of perfume or bake cookies, the aroma will gradually spread throughout your home. Once the molecules that make up the aroma are in about the same concentration everywhere, they continue to collide and bounce off one another.

Brain Power

Iodine is a test for starch. When added to a substance, iodine turns blue-black or purple if starch is present. Rice contains starch. What if rice is put in a sealed plastic bag and then that bag is placed in a jar filled with water mixed with iodine? Predict what would happen.

What is happening in these pictures as you look from left to right?

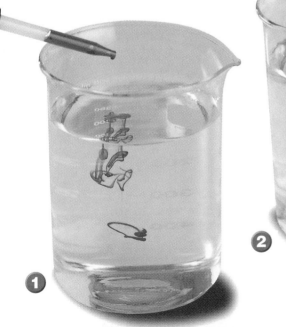

1

2

3

What Can Pass Through a Barrier?

The cell membrane is a kind of barrier, something like the tea bag in the Explore Activity. Cells get food, oxygen, and other substances from the environment. They also release wastes, such as the gas carbon dioxide. Substances move in and out of the cell through the cell membrane. Some kinds of molecules are able to pass through a cell membrane by diffusion.

That is, they move from areas of high concentration to low concentration.

Molecules of sugar, water, oxygen, and carbon dioxide do not require energy to move from high to low concentration. Such movement through cell membranes without the use of energy is called *passive transport*.

Other molecules, such as proteins and bacteria, are so large they can only enter the cell with the help of special processes that take place in the cell membrane.

Diffusion of oxygen and carbon dioxide through cell membrane

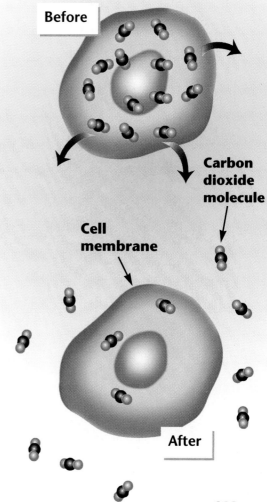

Oxygen In

Oxygen molecule

Before

Cell membrane

After

Carbon Dioxide Out

Before

Cell membrane

Carbon dioxide molecule

After

READING N DIAGRAMS

1. **DISCUSS** Do oxygen molecules go into or out of the cell?
2. **WRITE** Do carbon dioxide molecules go into or out of the cell?

How Does Water Pass Through the Cell Membrane?

Do you realize that water makes up about 70 to 95 percent of a living cell, depending on the kind of cell it is? The movement of water in and out of a cell is important in keeping the cell alive. The diffusion of water through a cell membrane is **osmosis** (oz mō′sis). Water molecules tend to move from an area of greater concentration to an area of lesser concentration. When the concentration of water molecules is the same on each side of a cell membrane, a state of *equilibrium*, or balance, is reached.

You can see examples of osmosis around you. Look at the two photographs. The plant in the second photo is the same as the one in the first photo after it has been watered. How can you explain the wilting of the leaves in the first photograph?

Most likely there is less water in the soil around the roots. Cells in the leaves and stems of the plant are not supplied with adequate water from the roots. The loss of water from the cell membranes causes them to shrink away from the cell. As a result the plant wilts. What other examples of osmosis can you think of?

Wilting occurs when more water leaves the cells than enters the cells.

Equilibrium is reached when water leaves the cells and enters the cells at the same rate.

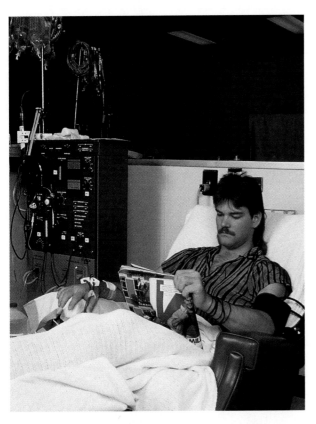

Hemodialysis is an effective treatment for patients who suffer from kidney disease. A treatment may take from two to four hours and is usually repeated two or three times a week.

How do cell activities such as osmosis, photosynthesis, and respiration affect you? If a cook sprinkles salt on a chicken breast prior to grilling, juices from the meat flow out of the meat by osmosis. The result can be a dry chicken breast.

For centuries people around the world have been putting fermentation to use. Yeasts are tiny organisms that produce the wastes carbon dioxide and alcohol during fermentation. Carbon dioxide is a gas. When yeast is added to dough, the carbon dioxide that forms makes the dough rise. The alcohol produced by yeast is found in wines and beers. It is also found in gasohol, a gasoline substitute for cars.

Certain bacteria carry out fermentation in milk and produce lactic acid and carbon dioxide. The tangy flavor of yogurt, sour cream, buttermilk, and cottage cheese comes from this process.

REVIEW

1. Describe the process that allows you to smell an open bottle of perfume.

2. What is the role of the cell membrane in moving substances in and out of the cell?

3. **COMPARE AND CONTRAST** Distinguish between passive transport and active transport.

4. How do cells get the energy they need to live?

5. **CRITICAL THINKING** *Analyze* How does a kidney machine use diffusion?

WHY IT MATTERS THINK ABOUT IT
Photosynthesis goes on in all cells that have chlorophyll—cells in plant leaves and stems, for example. Why is photosynthesis important for you?

WHY IT MATTERS WRITE ABOUT IT
How do you depend on plants? Why is it necessary for people to take care of plants—even plants that do not end up as food?

Biomass: Growing Energy

There are three ways to save natural resources.

1. Use less. Use energy-efficient cars and air refrigerators.
2. Reuse or recycle. Find new ways to use old materials again!
3. Grow new resources. Plant new trees to replace ones cut down.

Did you know that trees are a renewable energy resource? That's because we can always grow new ones. Coal, oil, and natural gas, however, are nonrenewable resources because it takes millions of years to make them.

People have used renewable resources for heat and light for centuries. Burning wood gave heat. Burning oil from plants or animal fat gave light. Plant energy resources are called biomass.

Coal replaced wood as fuel in England in the 1200s. A lot of the country's wood supply had already been used, but there was plenty of coal around. It was cheaper than wood, too!

Coal became even more important around 1800, after the invention of the steam engine. In the United States, early steam engines ran on wood, but in time

Making a Difference

Dr. Lang has discovered that about half of his cancer patients have changes in a tumor-suppressing gene. We know that tobacco smoke is one thing that causes changes in genes. Smokers who drink alcohol greatly increase their chances of getting cancer. Alcohol dissolves cancer-causing substances in the smoke, making it easier for them to reach cells in the mouth and throat. Once there they can cause changes that may lead to cancer.

Half a million Americans die of cancer every year. About 35 percent of those lives could be saved by early diagnosis and treatment.

DISCUSSION STARTER

1. Why does Dr. Lang focus on cells?

2. Why is the survival rate for cancer higher today than it's ever been?

To learn more about efforts to cure cancer, visit *www.mhschool.com/science* and select the keyword CANCER.

*inter*NET
CONNECTION

CHAPTER 3 REVIEW

SCIENCE WORDS

cell p.101

cell wall p.116

chloroplast p.116

chromosome p.114

diffusion p.128

fertilization p.145

meiosis p.144

mitosis p.141

organ p.105

organism p.105

organ system p.105

osmosis p.130

photosynthesis p.132

population p.106

USING SCIENCE WORDS

Number a paper from 1 to 10. Fill in 1 to 5 with words from the list above.

1. A bacterium is a one-celled ___?___.

2. A green body found in a plant cell is called a(n) ___?___.

3. The division of a nucleus when the chromosome number ends up unchanged is ___?___.

4. Food making in plants is ___?___.

5. An egg and sperm join during ___?___.

6–10. **Pick five words from the list above that were not used in 1 to 5, and use each in a sentence.**

UNDERSTANDING SCIENCE IDEAS

11. List in order words showing organization in an animal or plant.

12. List in order words showing organization in an ecosystem.

13. How are respiration and photosynthesis related?

14. How is meiosis different from mitosis?

15. Which parts of a plant cell are not found in an animal cell?

USING IDEAS AND SKILLS

16. Describe the populations that make up an environment—such as in a park or a desert. Describe how the populations interact.

17. **READING SKILL: COMPARE AND CONTRAST** How does the nucleus change while a cell divides?

18. When a cell divides, the chromosome number is divided in half. Is this statement always true, sometimes true, never true? Explain.

19. **MAKE A MODEL** What cell activity does data in this table relate to? How would you complete this table to show the process? Explain why.

Number of Cubes Used	Volume	Surface Area
1	1	6
8		

20. **THINKING LIKE A SCIENTIST** Which do you think will show diffusion—oil and water, warm water and cold water, ink and oil, ink and water? How would you test your answers?

PROBLEMS and PUZZLES

Small Enough? Molecules of a simple sugar will pass through a cell membrane easily, but molecules of a starch will not pass through easily. Which molecules do you think are larger?

starch

CHAPTER 4
CELLS AND THE KINGDOMS OF LIFE

What if you were on a tour of Earth? You would be amazed at the different kinds of living things you'd find. Do you recognize any living things shown here? Do they resemble any living things that you know?

How are all living things alike? How are living things different from each other? Is there a way of telling which living things are more alike than others?

This chapter will offer you many opportunities to draw conclusions.

WHY IT MATTERS

Classifying living things gives us a better understanding of their similarities and differences.

SCIENCE WORDS

kingdom one of the largest groups used to classify living things

phylum a main group within a kingdom, whose members share a main characteristic

species a group of similar organisms in a genus that can reproduce more of their own kind

scientific name a two-word term for a living thing, based on its classification

biodiversity the wide variety of life on Earth

Classifying Living Things

How can you tell a plant from an animal? A sea anemone lives in water and is attached to one spot. A euglena is green and moves through water. Would you identify each as a plant, an animal, or something else?

When you identify something as a plant, you are classifying it. How would you classify organisms as plants or animals? Do you think that all living things can fit into just these two groups?

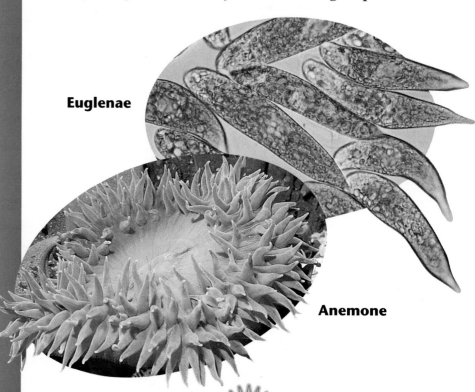

Euglenae

Anemone

EXPLORE

HYPOTHESIZE How would you classify all living things? How would you start— number of cells or ability to move? Write a hypothesis in your *Science Journal*. Test your ideas.

Investigate How Living Things Can Be Classified

Classify living things based on simple observations and facts.

PROCEDURES

1. OBSERVE Look at the organisms on pages 154–155. Read the descriptions carefully. In your *Science Journal,* list basic facts about each. Add to the facts from what you may know or what you may look up in books.

2. COMPARE AND CONTRAST Look at the organisms two at a time. How are they alike? Different? Record.

3. CLASSIFY Find ways to group the organisms. For example, you might group them based on whether they are one-celled or many-celled, or whether they take in food or make their own food.

CONCLUDE AND APPLY

1. CLASSIFY Combine your findings so that you have from three to five groups. What are your final groupings? What do the members of each group have in common?

2. EVALUATE Can you find more than one way to classify any organism? If so, why did you decide on one rather than another?

GOING FURTHER: Problem Solving

3. EXPERIMENT Add other organisms to your classification system. Study living specimens around you. You might observe organisms in a drop of aquarium (or pond) water.

MATERIALS

- illustrations on pages 154–155
- research books (optional)
- microscope (optional)
- coverslips, slides (optional)
- living specimens (optional)
- pond or aquarium water (optional)
- *Science Journal*

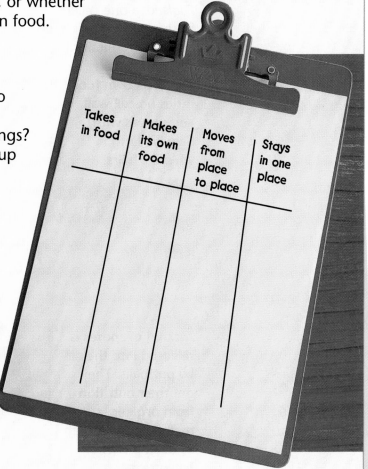

Takes in food	Makes its own food	Moves from place to place	Stays in one place

How Can Living Things Be Classified?

Which of these living things have you seen before? These pictures represent a wide variety of organisms from different environments on Earth. The Explore Activity used these living things to introduce classification.

4 Most kinds of bacteria move about and take in foods for energy and growth. Bacteria have cell walls and are found in three basic shapes—rodlike, spherical, and spiral.

1 *Paramecium* is a one-celled organism that lives in fresh or stagnant water. It is covered with cilia, tiny hairs that beat, helping it move and take in food.

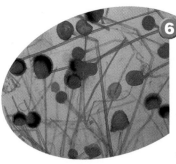

5 A mushroom grows when the cap breaks through the soil. A mushroom has no chlorophyll and cannot make its own food. It takes in nutrients from its surroundings.

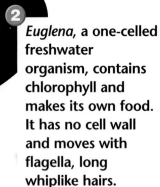

2 *Euglena*, a one-celled freshwater organism, contains chlorophyll and makes its own food. It has no cell wall and moves with flagella, long whiplike hairs.

6 Bread molds grow on bread that has been left in a warm, damp, dark place. These molds have short threadlike filaments that extend down into the bread and digest starches.

3 A cloud of spores is released into the air by puffballs. They get their nutrition from organic material in soil, such as dead plants or fallen trees.

7 Mosses grow in large groups that spread out like mats. They have short stems that lift delicate leaves above the ground. The leaves are generally about one cell thick.

8 *Elodea* is often called waterweed or ditch moss. Its stems can reach lengths of up to 1.1 meters (3.5 feet). Its flowers are small and its fruit ripen under water.

9 Geraniums have colorful flowers with five overlapping petals. Their roots absorb moisture from the soil and anchor the plants.

10 Hermit crabs live in and drag shells that have been cast off by other animals, such as sea snails.

11 Hamsters dig long burrows underground. Their cheek pouches are used for storing and carrying food.

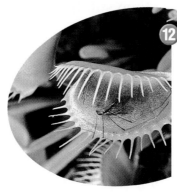

12 Hinged lobes at the edge of each leaf of a Venus's-flytrap are lined with sensory hairs. When prey comes into contact with the hairs, the lobes fold together, trapping the prey.

13 A goldfish's color comes from structures below colorless scales. Goldfish take in oxygen through gills.

14 Locomotion in most snails happens when contractions occur along the bottom of a muscular foot. When disturbed the snail can withdraw into its spiral shell. Snails feed off dead and decaying matter.

READING N CHARTS

1. **DISCUSS** Which of these living things are most alike? Explain.
2. **WRITE** Which of these living things are most different? Explain.

How Many Groups Are There?

Why do scientists classify living things? About 350 B.C. the Greek philosopher Aristotle classified living things into two groups—plants and animals. He was trying to make order or sense out of the variety of living things he studied. He then subdivided "animals" based on where they lived (land, water, or air) and their behavior. Plants were sorted into three smaller groups—herbs, shrubs, and trees.

Scientists used "animals" and "plants" as the two **kingdoms** of life until the 1800s. Kingdoms are the largest groups used to classify living things. Since Aristotle the kingdoms have been divided into many smaller groups based on how similar organisms are.

For example, the animal kingdom is divided into several **phyla** (fī′lə) (singular, *phylum*). All members of a phylum share at least one important structure or other characteristic. For example, elephants and earthworms all belong to the animal kingdom. But elephants have a backbone. Earthworms do not. All animals with backbones are grouped into a phylum called Chordata. This phylum includes seals, dogs, fishes, and humans. Earthworms are grouped in a phylum with leeches and sandworms.

TWO KINGDOMS

ANIMALS	PLANTS
• move about by swimming, crawling, walking • take in food by eating	• are rooted to the ground, don't move about • make their own food

THE ANIMAL KINGDOM

PHYLUM CHORDATA, the vertebrates, includes all animals with a backbone.

All other phlya have no backbone.

156

What Smaller Groups Do We Use?

A phylum is divided into smaller groups called *classes*. For example, the class Mammalia includes all animals that have fur or hair and produce milk for their young.

Members of a class that have the most in common are put into smaller groups called *orders*. The most similar members of an order are grouped into a *family*. The most similar family members are grouped into a *genus*.

The most similar members of a genus belong to a **species**. All members of a species can mate and reproduce more of their own kind. A species has the most similar members in a kingdom.

READING N CHARTS

1. DISCUSS What animals are mammals?
2. DISCUSS What animals are carnivores?

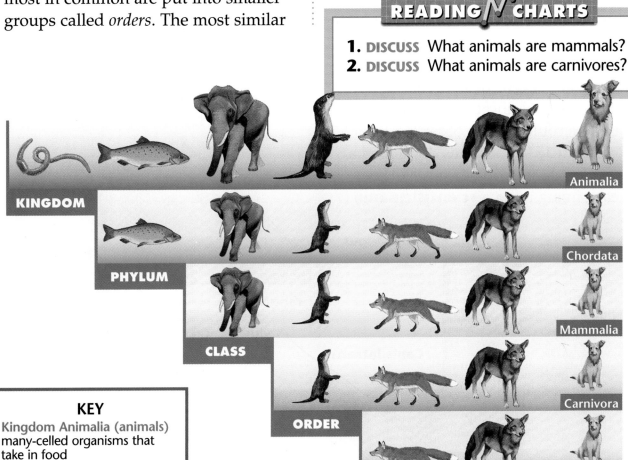

KINGDOM — Animalia

PHYLUM — Chordata

CLASS — Mammalia

ORDER — Carnivora

FAMILY — Canidae

GENUS — *Canis*

SPECIES — *Canis familiaris*

KEY

Kingdom Animalia (animals) many-celled organisms that take in food

Phylum Chordata (chordates) animals with a backbone, a rodlike support structure

Class Mammalia (mammals) chordates that nourish their young with milk and have fur

Order Carnivora (carnivores) mammals with sharp teeth and claws for eating meat

Family Canidae carnivores with coarse fur, long limbs, claws that do not pull in, eyes with rounded pupils

Genus *Canis* dogs, wolves, coyotes, jackals

Species *Canis familiaris* dogs

Brain Power

Look at the classification chart. What animal is not included as you go from each larger to each smaller level? Why is it not included?

157

How Do We Name Living Things?

Who developed the idea of dividing a kingdom into smaller and smaller groups? The idea comes from Carolus Linnaeus, a Swedish scientist. Linnaeus lived in the 1700s. He did not have the powerful microscopes of today that reveal more detail about cells of an organism. He based his classification on structures that he could readily observe.

About 1735, Linnaeus developed a way of naming organisms. He gave each living thing a **scientific name** based on its classification—that is, its genus and species. Since many of the same organisms in different parts of the world have different common names, Latin is used in scientific names to make it easier to understand. The scientific name for timber wolf is *Canis lupus*. The name comes from the genus *Canis* and the species *lupus*. The genus name always starts with a capital letter. Why was it important to come up with a scientific name?

Canis lupus

Canis latrans

Canis familiaris

Wolves, coyotes, and dogs belong to the same genus. But they are different species.

CLASSIFICATION OF THREE SPECIES

	DOMESTIC CAT	BOBCAT	HUMAN
Kingdom	Animalia	Animalia	Animalia
Phylum	Chordata	Chordata	Chordata
Class	Mammalia	Mammalia	Mammalia
Order	Carnivora	Carnivora	Primates
Family	Felidae	Felidae	Hominidae
Genus	*Felis*	*Lynx*	*Homo*
Species	*catus*	*rufus*	*sapiens*

READING CHARTS

1. **DISCUSS** Which of these organisms are chordates (members of phylum Chordata)?
2. **WRITE** Which of these organisms are mammals?
3. **WRITE** Which two organisms are more closely related?

How Are Members of a Group Alike and Different?

Organisms in a phylum are grouped according to body structure. Both humans and dolphins have backbones, which makes them members of the same phylum. As organisms are grouped further into classes, orders, families, and genera, more similarity exists among the organism's body structures.

Body structure often shows that living things may have had a common ancestor. For example, the flippers of the walrus, the sea lion, and the seal provide evidence of a common ancestor. In some cases two species that seem very different may be closely related. The flippers of the whale and the arms of the human are similar structures that suggest a common ancestry. Fossils are often evidence of that ancestry.

You learned in Topic 2 that living things are made up of carbon compounds, such as proteins. Organisms that have many proteins in common are closely related. Guinea pigs were once grouped with mice and squirrels in the same order—rodents. When the proteins of a guinea pig were compared with those of other rodents and other types of mammals, scientist concluded that the guinea pig did not show a common ancestry. Now it is classified in a group of its own.

By comparing structures closely, scientist began to realize that more than two kingdoms were needed to classify organisms. In the 1600s, when microscopes first revealed one-celled organisms, scientists began to see that these organisms were different from many-celled organisms. By the late 1800s, scientists knew that one-celled organisms did not belong in the plant and animal kingdoms.

Horses, tapirs, and rhinoceroses belong to a group of mammals with three toes. They also have teeth for grinding and crushing hard plant material.

159

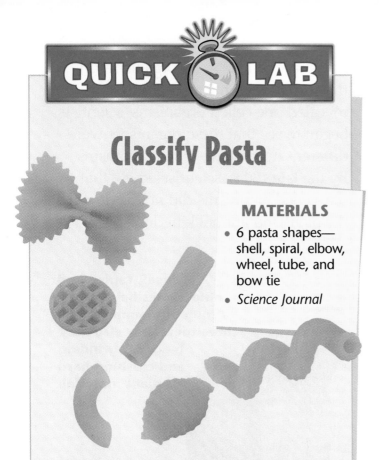

QUICK LAB

Classify Pasta

MATERIALS
- 6 pasta shapes—shell, spiral, elbow, wheel, tube, and bow tie
- *Science Journal*

PROCEDURES

1. COMPARE The six shapes belong to one large group of pasta that can be subdivided into smaller groups. What traits will you use to divide the pasta into two groups? Write your ideas in your *Science Journal.*

2. CLASSIFY Next, further divide each of the two groups on the basis of the traits you observe.

CONCLUDE AND APPLY

1. How did you divide the pasta into the first two groups? What traits did you use to make your classification?

2. How did you further divide the groups? What other traits led you to your decision?

3. EXPERIMENT Can you find another way to classify the pasta shapes?

How Else Are Living Things Grouped?

A substance called DNA is found in the chromosomes of all living things. DNA is similar for all living things, yet each living thing has a distinct pattern of the pieces that make up DNA. DNA helps in identifying an organism, almost like fingerprints. The more closely related organisms are, the more similar their DNA is. Members of the same species have very similar DNA.

Based on appearance the horseshoe crab used to be grouped in the same phylum as crabs and other crustaceans. Then it was discovered that its blood was more like that of a spider. Now the horse-shoe crab is grouped with spiders.

Giant pandas were classified with bears until the 1980s. Then they were grouped with raccoons. Some scientists now classify the giant panda and the red panda in their own family, *Ailuridae.*

WHY IT MATTERS

Classification gives us a better understanding of similarities and differences between organisms. You can now look up the scientific names of animals or plants you know and tell which are more closely related. Scientists are still classifying organisms they discover on mountaintops and in ocean depths.

These tube worms live at deep ocean bottoms.

REVIEW

1. *Euglena* is a one-celled organism that moves on its own and has chloroplasts. Why would it have been difficult to classify in Aristotle's time?

2. The scientific name for the bobcat is *Lynx rufus* and for the lynx is *Lynx canadensis*. How do their names indicate that they are related? How are they different?

3. Why is the two-word naming system useful to scientists?

4. **CLASSIFY** Humans belong to the class Mammalia. How do humans fit into the chart on page 157?

5. **CRITICAL THINKING** *Analyze* How do scientists classify living things?

WHY IT MATTERS THINK ABOUT IT
Humans have arms with hands and fingers. How does this help us? What other organisms have similar features?

WHY IT MATTERS WRITE ABOUT IT
Mammals include horses, pigs, deer, dolphins, elephants, bats, wolves, dogs, cats, rodents, and primates (monkeys, apes, and humans). Describe the similarities and differences of some of these animals.

Finding Your Root Words

Swedish scientist Carolus Linnaeus invented a method to classify living things into a logical system. In his system the scientific name for each plant and animal is composed of two words, such as *Felis catus* (house cat). The first word is the name of the genus, and the second word is the name of the species.

Linnaeus chose Latin words because the scientists of his day used that language. (He even changed his own name from von Linné to the Latin Linnaeus!)

Many other science terms are based on Latin, and some are based on ancient Greek. A Latin or Greek word is often the root of a longer word. The root indicates the basic meaning of the word.

Some words have two roots. For example, *biology* has two Greek roots. One root is *bio*, meaning "life," and the other

is *logy*, meaning "the study of." Thus *biology* means "the study of life."

Besides being a combination of two or more root words, a science word may have a prefix or a suffix. A prefix is attached to the beginning of the root word. A suffix is attached to the end. For example, adding the Latin prefix *re-*, meaning "again," to *produce* makes it *reproduce*. Adding the suffix *-ic* to *organ* makes it *organic* and changes the word from a noun to an adjective.

GIRAFFE
Giraffa camelopardalis

Language Arts Link

Here are some roots, prefixes, and suffixes used in science and their meanings. Can you name words that use these roots, prefixes, and suffixes?

WORD PART	MEANING
chlor-	green
chromo-	color
cyto-	cell
gen-	birth
micro-	tiny
mito-	thread
-osis	process
-plast	particle
-some	body

CHEETAH
Acinonyx jubatus

LEOPARD
Panthera pardus

TIGER
Panthera tigris

LION
Panthero leo

DISCUSSION STARTER

1. Why did early scientists use Latin words to describe new discoveries?

2. What would be the name for a "green body"? A "tiny particle"? A "cell process"?

COUGAR
Felis puma

HOUSE CAT
Felis catus

To learn more about root words, visit **www.mhschool.com/science** and select the keyword ROOTS.

*inter***NET**
CONNECTION

163

Topic 6
LIFE SCIENCE

WHY IT MATTERS

Every organism plays an important role in the life of other organisms.

SCIENCE WORDS

microbe a living thing so small that it can be seen only with a microscope

virus a microscopic particle made of hereditary material and a protein coat, which can reproduce inside a living cell

The Kingdoms of Life

What do a frog, a parakeet, a turtle, a cat, a goldfish, and a dog have in common? What is something they all do or all have?

They all belong to the animal kingdom. Each has a backbone. This means they all belong to the phylum Chordata. However, they belong to different classes. Using this simplified classification key, how would you classify a frog, a parakeet, a turtle, a cat, and a goldfish?

All Animals with Backbones

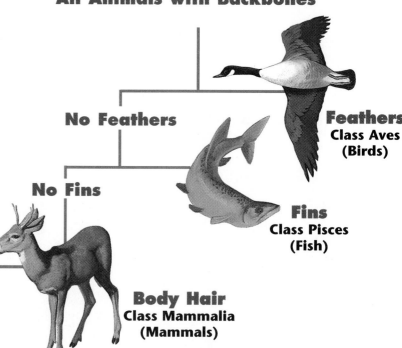

No Feathers

Feathers
Class Aves
(Birds)

No Fins

Fins
Class Pisces
(Fish)

No Body Hair

Body Hair
Class Mammalia
(Mammals)

No Scales
No claws on toes
Class Amphibia
(Amphibians)

Dry Scales
Claws on toes
Class Reptilia
(Reptiles)

EXPLORE

HYPOTHESIZE How can you tell the differences and similarities between very similar organisms—such as trees? Write a hypothesis in your *Science Journal.* Test your ideas.

164

Investigate How to Classify Living Things

Use a classification key to compare and contrast leaves.

MATERIALS
- *Science Journal*

LEAF KEY

1a. Leaf blade deeply divided . . . . .Green Ash
1b. Leaf blade not deeply divided . . . . . . .Go to 2

2a. Leaf blade long and narrow . . . . . .Black Willow
2b. Leaf blade not long and narrow . . . . . .Go to 3

3a. Leaf blade not cut into lobes . . . . .Go to 4
3b. Leaf blade cut into lobes . . . . .Go to 5

4a. Base flat, leaf heart-shaped . . . . . .Cottonwood
4b. Base uneven . . . . .American Elm

5a. Lobes rounded . . . . .White Oak
5b. Lobes pointed . . . . .Silver Maple

Lobes

A

PROCEDURES

COMPARE Write the letters A–F in your *Science Journal*. For each letter use the leaf key to write a name.

B

C

CONCLUDE AND APPLY

1. COMPARE AND CONTRAST
Which leaves have the most in common? On what did you base your answer?

Lobes

E

GOING FURTHER: Apply

2. CLASSIFY Make your own classification key to compare and contrast similar things. For example, insects have wings or no wings, tails or no tails. You might also make a key for cars, rooms at school, pizza toppings, or whatever you choose.

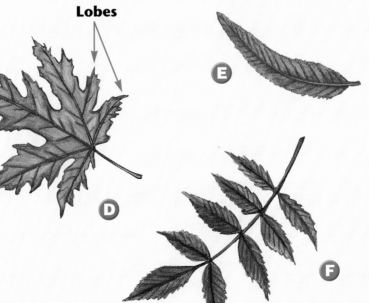

D

F

How Can You Classify Living Things?

How would you classify members of the animal kingdom? Is the organism many celled or one celled? Does it make food, take in (eat) food, or absorb food? If it is one celled, does it have a cell wall? Does it have a true nucleus or just a nuclear material without a membrane around it?

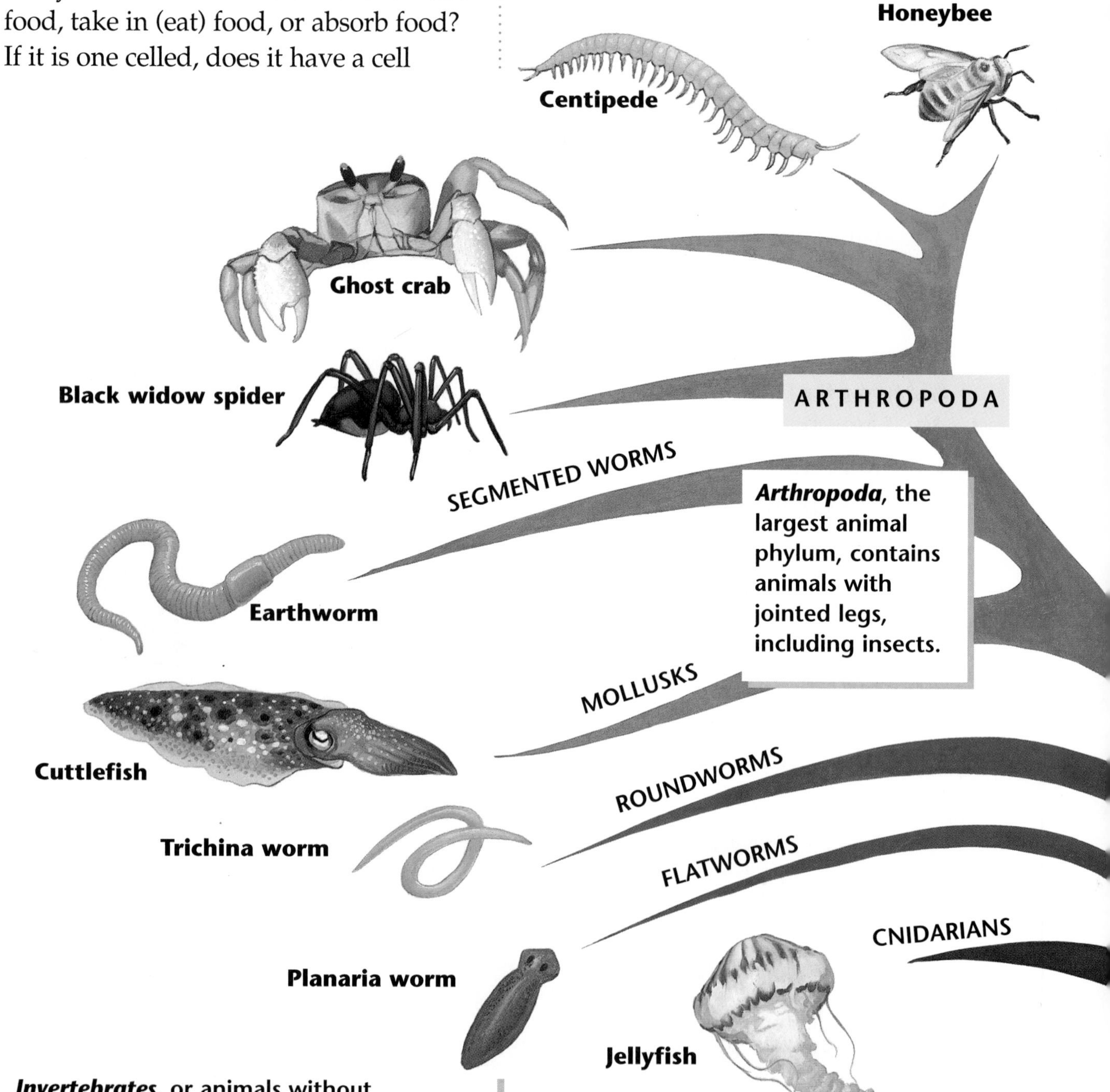

Centipede

Honeybee

Ghost crab

Black widow spider

ARTHROPODA

SEGMENTED WORMS

Arthropoda, the largest animal phylum, contains animals with jointed legs, including insects.

Earthworm

MOLLUSKS

Cuttlefish

ROUNDWORMS

Trichina worm

FLATWORMS

CNIDARIANS

Planaria worm

Jellyfish

Invertebrates, or animals without backbones, make up about 97 percent of the animal kingdom.

166

Vertebrates, or animals with backbones, include members of the phylum Chordata—fish, amphibians, reptiles, birds, and mammals.

CHARACTERISTICS OF ANIMALS

- many-celled organisms
- cells have true nucleus; no cell wall
- eat and digest other organisms
- most can move from place to place
- have tissues organized into organs and organ systems

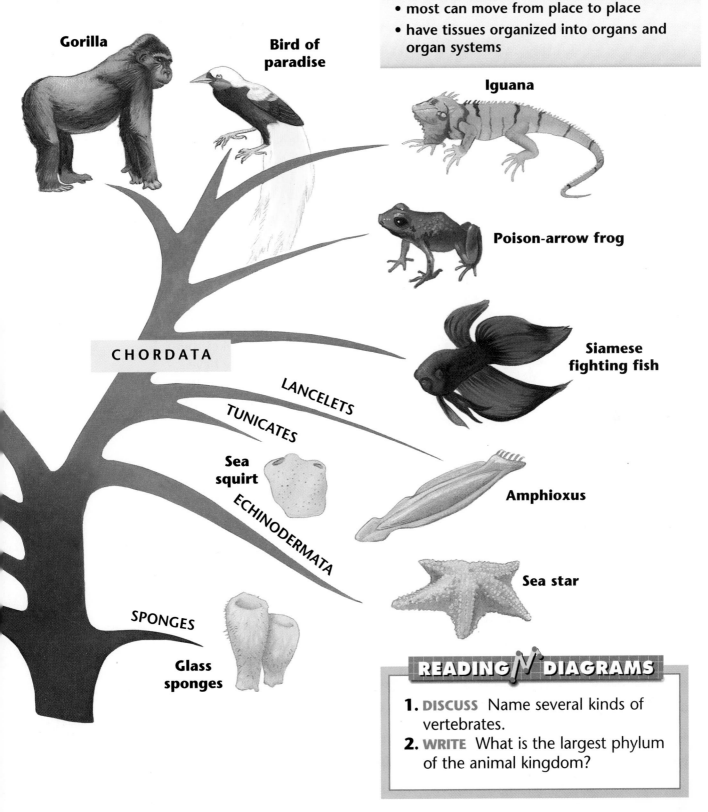

Gorilla

Bird of paradise

Iguana

Poison-arrow frog

Siamese fighting fish

CHORDATA

LANCELETS

TUNICATES

Sea squirt

ECHINODERMATA

Amphioxus

Sea star

SPONGES

Glass sponges

READING *N* DIAGRAMS

1. DISCUSS Name several kinds of vertebrates.

2. WRITE What is the largest phylum of the animal kingdom?

How Is the Plant Kingdom Organized?

Plants are grouped into divisions, rather than phyla. What do all plants have in common?

CHARACTERISTICS OF PLANTS

- many-celled organism
- many cells have chlorophyll—in light, they make their food (and produce oxygen)
- cells have walls; have true nucleus
- roots or rootlike structures anchor the plant and absorb water

FLOWERING PLANTS reproduce by seeds that develop inside a protective chamber, called an ovary. Like ferns and cone-bearing plants, they have true roots, stems, and leaves.

HORSETAILS are usually found in moist, sandy places. They contain sand, which makes them feel rough. They have tiny scalelike leaves that form rings around the stem.

MOSSES were among the first plants to live on land. They have no special tissues for transporting water or nutrients. Some mosses have a stalk and a capsule, where spores, or reproductive cells, are found. They do not reproduce by producing seeds.

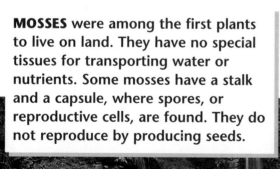

CONE-BEARING PLANTS reproduce with seeds. They carry their seeds in cones, rather than in pods or fruit. Like ferns they have true roots, stems, and leaves. Examples include redwoods, pines, firs, spruces, and hemlocks.

FERNS have special tissues to transport water and nutrients. This allows them to grow taller than mosses. Like mosses ferns are seedless plants.

CLUB MOSSES, unlike true mosses, have true roots, stems, and leaves. Club mosses grow mainly in damp, shady areas. Some are found in deserts and on mountains.

READING N DIAGRAMS

1. **DISCUSS** Name a seedless plant.
2. **WRITE** What are the two main kinds of seed plants? Describe their differences in a paragraph.

What's in the Fungus Kingdom?

Fungi (fun'jī) (singular, *fungus*—fung'gəs) are grouped into divisions, rather than phyla. This kingdom includes **microbes** (mī'krōbz), living things that are so small they can be seen only with microscopes. It also includes larger organisms. What do all fungi have in common?

Mold on bread is a microbe that is part of the fungus kingdom.

Rusts and smuts can cause severe damage to crops.

Mushrooms come in many sizes and shapes. The part of the mushroom that rises above ground is the fruiting body. The growing, vegetative part lies underground in the form of a mass of dense, tangled threads.

History of Science

American scientist Herbert Copeland adds a fourth kingdom, Monera, for organisms with no nucleus.

German scientist Ernst Haeckel suggests putting one-celled creatures in a third kingdom, called Protista.

Scientists study the Monera kingdom closely and replace it with two new kingdoms: Eubacteria, or "true bacteria," include those that cause disease and decay; Archaebacteria, or "ancient bacteria," produce energy without using oxygen.

1750s　　**1866**　　**1956**　　**1959**　　**1990s**

Carolus Linnaeus simplifies the names of plants and animals into two words, genus and species.

Robert Whittaker suggests a fifth kingdom, called Fungi. These organisms look like plants, can't move, and can't make their own food.

DISCUSSION STARTER

1. What kind of information do scientists need before they can classify an organism?

2. If a seventh kingdom is ever added, what type of organisms do you think will be in it?

To learn more about kingdoms, visit **www.mhschool.com/science** and select the keyword KING.

*inter*NET
CONNECTION

177

There are patterns in the way you and other living things grow.

SCIENCE WORDS

fission a kind of asexual reproduction in which one parent cell divides into two offspring cells

budding a kind of asexual reproduction in which a new organism develops from a bump (bud) on the side of the parent

conjugation a kind of sexual reproduction in which two parent cells join and exchange material before they divide

spore a cell that can develop into an adult organism without fertilization

metamorphosis the changes of body form that some animals go through in their life cycle

Living Things Reproduce and Grow

How do people grow and change? Think of a plant starting with a seed. How does the plant grow and change?

All organisms have a life cycle—a cycle of beginning, growing, reproducing, and dying. This cycle happens in many ways. For example, most plants reproduce sexually, that is, from two parent cells that form a seed.

These seed plants also reproduce asexually. How are they reproducing?

EXPLORE

HYPOTHESIZE How can you tell if a microbe is reproducing sexually or asexually? Write a hypothesis in your *Science Journal*. Test your ideas.

Investigate How Microbes Reproduce

Observe and compare yeast cells to tell how they are reproducing.

MATERIALS
- yeast mixture
- dropper
- microscope
- microscope slide
- coverslip
- *Science Journal*

PROCEDURES

1. Use a dropper to place a drop of the yeast mixture on the microscope slide.

2. **RECORD** Observe the slide under low power. In your *Science Journal*, draw what you see. Then turn to high power. Draw what you see.

CONCLUDE AND APPLY

1. **OBSERVE** Describe the yeast cells you observed.

2. **INTERPRET DATA** What type of reproduction is this? Explain your answer.

GOING FURTHER: Problem Solving

3. **EXPERIMENT** Design an experiment in which you test for each of the characteristic activities of life as described in Topic 1, page 100.

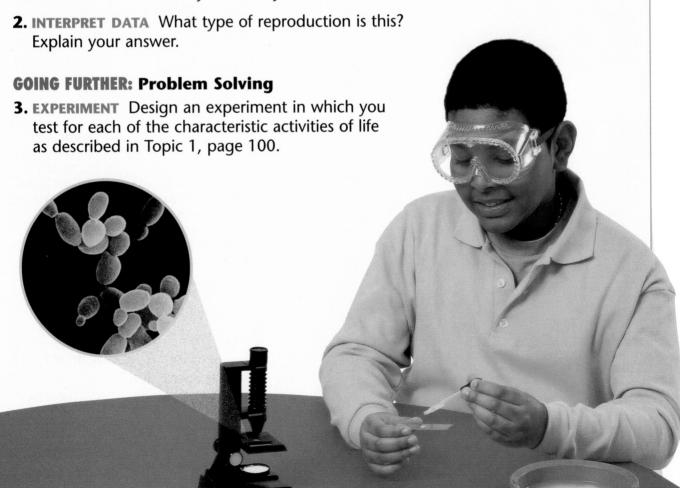

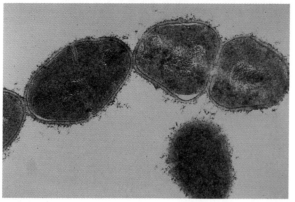

Fission in bacteria

How Do Microbes Reproduce?

The Explore Activity focused on the reproduction of yeast. The life cycle of many microbes involves only one parent cell. However, some microbes also reproduce from two parent cells.

Buds on yeast cells

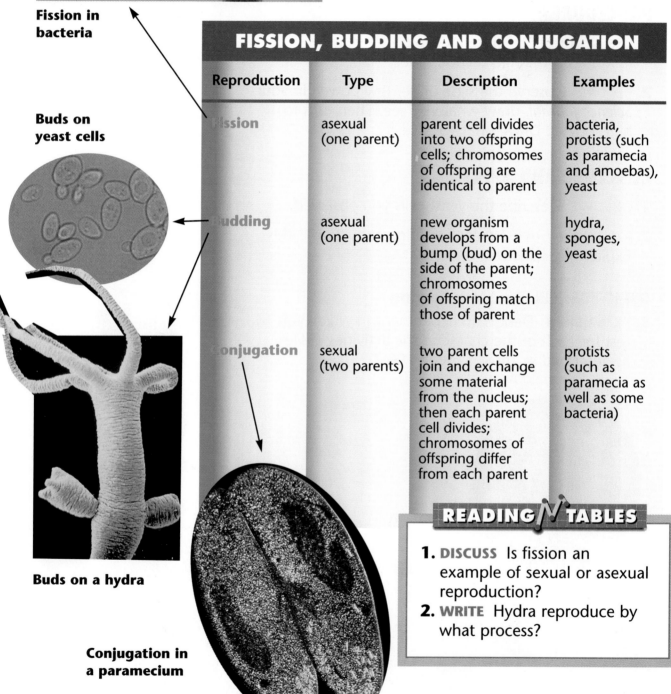

Buds on a hydra

Conjugation in a paramecium

FISSION, BUDDING AND CONJUGATION

Reproduction	Type	Description	Examples
Fission	asexual (one parent)	parent cell divides into two offspring cells; chromosomes of offspring are identical to parent	bacteria, protists (such as paramecia and amoebas), yeast
Budding	asexual (one parent)	new organism develops from a bump (bud) on the side of the parent; chromosomes of offspring match those of parent	hydra, sponges, yeast
Conjugation	sexual (two parents)	two parent cells join and exchange some material from the nucleus; then each parent cell divides; chromosomes of offspring differ from each parent	protists (such as paramecia as well as some bacteria)

READING TABLES

1. **DISCUSS** Is fission an example of sexual or asexual reproduction?
2. **WRITE** Hydra reproduce by what process?

How Does Bread Mold Reproduce?

Members of the fungus kingdom, such as bread molds and mushrooms reproduce by forming **spores**—tiny, asexual reproductive cells. A single spore can develop into an adult without fertilization by another cell. Ferns, mosses, and even bacteria can also reproduce by forming spores.

Spore case

Spores

Hyphae

The black fuzz you see on bread mold is actually hyphae—individual filaments that make up the body of the fungus. When an airborne spore lands on a piece of bread, it forms hyphae, which branch out over the bread's surface. The fruiting body at the tip of the mass of hyphae contains spores. It bursts when ripe to release spores from within.

The parts of the fungus you see on moldy fruit are the reproductive structures that contain the spores. A mushroom is actually the reproductive part of the fungus that grows under the ground. The spores are found beneath the cap.

You can look at a fresh mushroom from a grocery store. Just pull off the cap. Use a hand lens to observe the spores on the underneath side of the cap. You can pull the stem apart to see the hyphae. Draw your observations.

Mushroom

Spores

Spore-producing hyphae

Stalk

What Cycle Do Seed Plants Have?

The life cycle of most plants you know begins with the formation of a seed. How is a seed made? A seed is the result of fertilization. This occurs when a pollen grain, which carries sperm, touches the egg-producing organ of a plant.

Plant Life Cycles

Seed plants do not all have the same cycle. Plants like tomatoes grow, reproduce, and die all in one year. Such plants are called annuals.

Some plants, such as carrots, are biennials. They produce leaves and food one year, and reproduce and die the next year.

Most trees and shrubs are perennials. They live from one year to the next and continue to grow and reproduce regularly.

1 **GERMINATION**
A seed *germinates*.
That is, it sprouts
a root, a stem,
and a leaf.

2 **GROWTH AND REPRODUCTION**
The young plant, or *seedling*,
pops through the ground.
With the right conditions, it
grows and reproduces.

3 **STARTING OVER**
After reproducing, annual
and biennial plants die.
Although reproduction is
often the final stage for a
mature plant, that doesn't
mean the end of things.
The seeds, spores, and new
plants that a parent plant
produces start the life
cycle all over again.

Growth and development involves physical changes as well as social and emotional changes.

What Life Cycles Do Animals Have?

Animals grow up in very different ways from plants. The life cycle of a fruit fly is different from that of a human. Your own life cycle is different from that of a cat or a dog. Some animals, such as fruit flies, hatch from eggs. Other animals are born alive. Below are the stages animals such as humans, gorillas, and whales go through.

Birth

Bears, lions, and humans are all born looking like small adults. Even young birds, fish, and reptiles, such as snakes, turtles, and alligators, hatch out of their eggs looking pretty much like their parents, except for their color and size.

Growth, Development, and Reproduction

Childhood and adolescence in humans are the periods of growth and development. As animals get bigger, they learn to survive. Adulthood is a time of reproduction and then aging. Most animals need both a male and a female to reproduce.

Death

Some animals die after reproducing. Others live many years after they lose the ability to reproduce. Humans and elephants usually fall into the second category.

Brain Power

What are the ways in which a person's body changes during his or her life? Do you think that these changes fall into any useful categories? If so, what are those categories?

How Do Some Animals Change as They Grow?

Have you ever seen an animal change the way it looks? When animals change from one form to a completely different form during their life cycle, it is called **metamorphosis**.

LADYBUG LIFE CYCLE

Butterflies, mosquitoes, wasps, fireflies, ladybugs, and bees go through a *complete metamorphosis*, in four distinct stages.

1 Egg
Fertilized eggs are laid by the adult female ladybug.

2 Larva
An egg hatches into a larva. During this stage the young ladybug looks completely different from the adult. The larva eats and grows larger.

3 Pupa
The larva stops feeding and enters the pupa stage. It covers itself with a special case. During the pupa stage, larval tissue breaks down. Adult structures, such as wings, begin to form.

4 Adult
When the changes, or metamorphosis, are complete, the adult comes out of the pupa. The adult can reproduce to start a new life cycle.

GRASSHOPPER LIFE CYCLE

Some insects, such as grasshoppers, go through an *incomplete metamorphosis*, with only three stages.

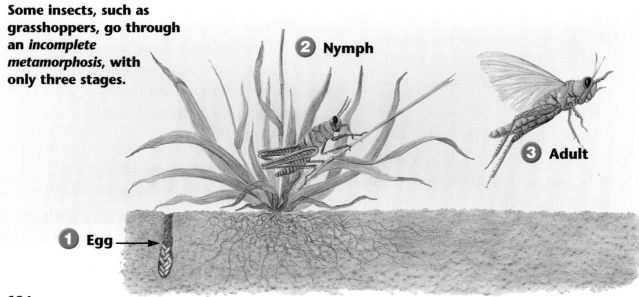

2 Nymph

3 Adult

1 Egg

FROG LIFE CYCLE

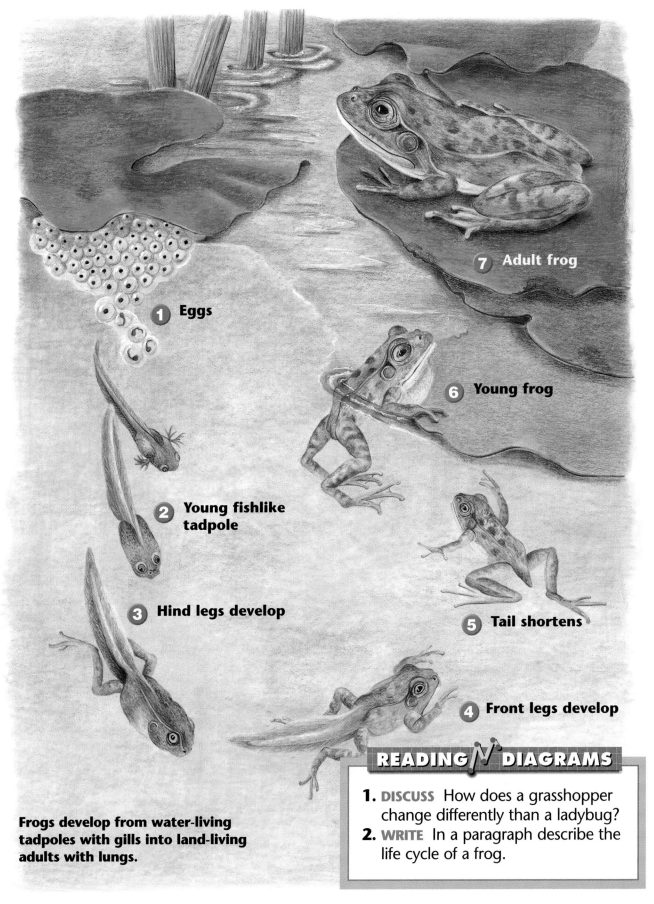

1 Eggs

7 Adult frog

6 Young frog

2 Young fishlike tadpole

3 Hind legs develop

5 Tail shortens

4 Front legs develop

Frogs develop from water-living tadpoles with gills into land-living adults with lungs.

READING DIAGRAMS

1. **DISCUSS** How does a grasshopper change differently than a ladybug?
2. **WRITE** In a paragraph describe the life cycle of a frog.

QUICK LAB

Limiting the Growth of Bacteria

PROCEDURES

SAFETY
Wear goggles.

MATERIALS
- bouillon broth
- 2 small spoons
- 20 mL white vinegar
- salt
- 3 jars
- masking tape
- goggles
- *Science Journal*

1. Pour 50 mL of the prepared bouillon broth into each of three jars. Use the masking tape to label the first jar "salt," the second jar "vinegar," and the third jar "nothing."

2. **USE VARIABLES** To the first jar, add 1 spoonful of salt. To the second jar, add 1 spoonful of vinegar.

3. **COLLECT DATA** Place all three jars in a warm, dry place for three days. Then compare the appearance of the jars. Record your observations in your *Science Journal*.

CONCLUDE AND APPLY

1. **EXPERIMENT** What conditions were kept the same in the activity?

2. **USE VARIABLES** What condition was tested?

3. **DRAW CONCLUSIONS** How do you explain the differences among the jars?

4. **MAKE DECISIONS** How might salt or vinegar be used to preserve food?

How Can Bacteria Spoil Food?

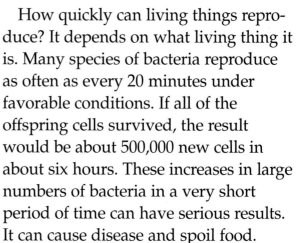

How quickly can living things reproduce? It depends on what living thing it is. Many species of bacteria reproduce as often as every 20 minutes under favorable conditions. If all of the offspring cells survived, the result would be about 500,000 new cells in about six hours. These increases in large numbers of bacteria in a very short period of time can have serious results. It can cause disease and spoil food.

Bacteria can grow in food that is not protected by any kind of preservative. There are many bacteria, molds, and yeasts in foods that can cause spoilage. Canning, pasteurization, freezing, and dehydration are ways to kill microbes or keep them from growing.

High temperatures usually kill most bacteria. Canning is a process that uses high temperatures to kill bacteria and other microorganisms. By sealing foods in airtight packages, microbes are kept out of the food.

USING IDEAS AND SKILLS

16. Describe how a human grows. How is growth measured?

17. Why do all living things need food? What are some other basic needs?

18. Create a scene with at least one member from each kingdom.

19. List the six main activities of living things. Which is the most important?

20. MAKE A MODEL Blood is pumped by our circulatory system. It gets filtered through our kidneys. What materials would you need to build a model of this system?

21. What are the two types of asexual reproduction? Give examples.

22. Describe each stage of complete metamorphosis. Give examples.

23. Describe how the nonliving parts of an ecosystem can determine what can live there. Give examples.

THINKING LIKE A SCIENTIST

24. How do you know when a cell is dividing? What happens to the chromosomes?

25. CLASSIFY A new organism is many celled and eats food. It has a backbone, gives its young milk, and eats meat. Classify it.

interNET CONNECTION

For help in reviewing this unit, visit: *www.mhschool.com/science*

WRITING IN YOUR JOURNAL

HOW SCIENTISTS WORK
Louis Pasteur, Anton van Leeuwenhoek, Carolus Linnaeus, and Robert Hooke are scientists mentioned in this unit. What do you think made them great scientists? How were they able to make the discoveries they made? How did these discoveries help us?

SCIENCE IN YOUR LIFE
Sometimes a natural disaster can totally change an ecosystem. Can you think of examples of these kinds of disasters? Have any happened in recent history? Have they happened near where you live?

PRODUCT ADS
Food labels now list amounts of calories, fat, carbohydrates, and protein, all terms discussed in this unit. Pick a few of your favorite foods and study the labels. What do the amounts tell you about the foods you are eating?

Design your own Experiment

If you introduce a new organism into an ecosystem, what changes might take place? Make a hypothesis. Design an experiment that introduces a new organism into an ecosystem, and observe the changes.

PROBLEMS and PUZZLES

Cell City Want Ads

Imagine a cell as a city. The nucleus would be city hall. The mitochondria would be power plants, and vacuoles would be storage bins. Write a want ad for a job in one of the cell's structures, like the one shown. Display your want ad for the class to observe.

Help Wanted

CHLOROPLAST WORKERS

Top-paying positions in the cell's FOOD FACTORY. You will take simple raw materials, water and carbon dioxide, and transform them into top-quality SUGARS! Qualifications: Work in bright sunlight required. You must be green. Hours: Summer: 12-hour-plus days. Nights and winters off. Send resume to THE NUCLEUS, in care of the PLANT CELL.

Shrink Wrap

Seawater is salty. Can we use salty water to water plants? What effect would salty water have on plant cells? Make a prediction. Test your ideas by observing some plant cells—like a very thin section of onion skin or an *Elodea* leaf—under a microscope. First use fresh water to make a wet mount. Then tap it dry, and add salty water. What happens? How do you think it is possible for some plants to live in seawater?

Classified Products

What if you were planning to open a store—a record store, a toy store, a clothes store, or even a department store? Classify your products into large and smaller groupings in ways that help people find what they are looking for. How would you set up a store directory to guide people to the areas with the products they want? Draw a floor plan for your store to show how you would display your products. Use a computer to help organize your floor plan.

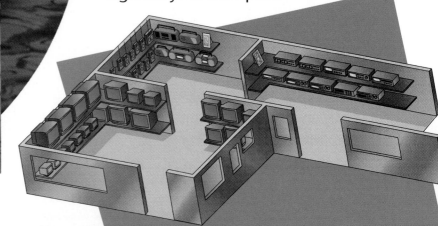

DISCUSSION STARTER

1. How could you use Aristotle's idea of how a thrown object moves through space to explain why it will eventually slow down and stop?

2. How could you use Newton's concept of inertia and the force of gravity to explain the motion of a pendulum after it's started?

To learn more about the laws of motion, visit *www.mhschool.com/science* and select the keyword MOVING.

*inter***NET**
CONNECTION

Topic 3
PHYSICAL SCIENCE

WHY IT MATTERS

The laws of motion help engineers build rockets.

SCIENCE WORDS

momentum the mass of an object multiplied by its velocity

More of Newton's Laws

What do you think it takes to get a building to move? The Empire in New York City, an old theater weighing over 3,000 tons, had to be moved down a city block to make way for a new hotel. How do you think it was done?

What if you had to move a house across town? Would it be easier if you took the furniture out? Why or why not? What else could you do to make the move easier?

To answer think about what it takes to get any object moving from rest—a crate, a car, a desk. How can you make the task easier?

EXPLORE

HYPOTHESIZE Moving something from rest means there is an acceleration. What determines how quickly something accelerates, or speeds up? Write a hypothesis in your *Science Journal*. How might you test your ideas?

EXPLORE ACTIVITY

Investigate What Affects Acceleration

MATH LINK

Experiment with two variables, the mass of a car and the force on the car, to see how they affect acceleration.

MATERIALS

- balloon-powered toy car
- 4 nickels
- meterstick
- tape
- lightweight cardboard
- scissors
- *Science Journal*

PROCEDURES

1. Make three balloon-inflation gauges of different sizes (12 cm, 8 cm, and 4 cm in diameter) by cutting the cardboard into U shapes.

2. Mark a starting line by sticking the tape on a smooth, level floor or a table surface 2 m long.

3. **MEASURE** Blow up the balloon to 12 cm using the 12-cm gauge. Place the toy car, attached to the inflated balloon, on the starting line. Let the air rush out, and measure how far the car travels before coming to a stop. Record your results in your *Science Journal.*

4. **COLLECT DATA** Use a piece of tape to attach a nickel to the car. Repeat step 3 for one nickel, two nickels, three nickels, and four nickels.

5. **COLLECT DATA** Repeat steps 3 and 4 using the 8-cm gauge and the 4-cm gauge.

CONCLUDE AND APPLY

1. **ANALYZE** What happened to the acceleration of the car as more mass was added?

2. **ANALYZE** What happened to the acceleration of the car as more force was used?

GOING FURTHER: Problem Solving

3. **INFER** Why do race car drivers try to reduce the weight of their cars as much as possible?

4. **ANALYZE** How could you make a car carrying four nickels accelerate as fast as one with none?

What Affects Acceleration?

The diagram on this page shows a simple experiment using rubber bands stretched by the same amount and a small cart loaded with books. By using two rubber bands, you can double the force, and by using twice as many books, you can increase the mass of the cart.

After studying the picture, can you see that the cart travels farthest when the force is greatest and the number of books is smallest? This tells us that a large force on an object with small mass results in a large acceleration. In contrast the distance traveled by the cart is least when the smallest force is applied and the most books are placed on the cart. As a result we know that a small force applied to an object with large mass causes a small acceleration.

Rubber bands exerting a force on a cart

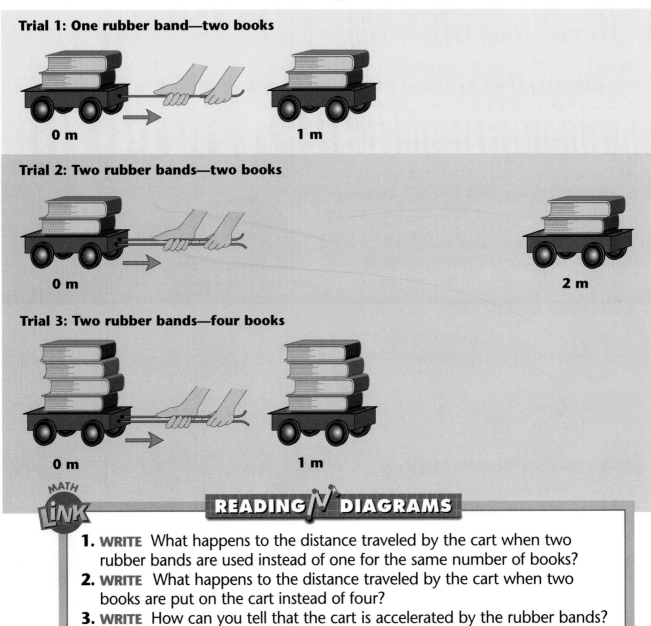

Trial 1: One rubber band—two books

0 m   1 m

Trial 2: Two rubber bands—two books

0 m   2 m

Trial 3: Two rubber bands—four books

0 m   1 m

MATH LINK

READING N DIAGRAMS

1. **WRITE** What happens to the distance traveled by the cart when two rubber bands are used instead of one for the same number of books?
2. **WRITE** What happens to the distance traveled by the cart when two books are put on the cart instead of four?
3. **WRITE** How can you tell that the cart is accelerated by the rubber bands?

How Are Force and Mass Related?

If you are moving a house or pushing a bookcase, how can you make the job easier? Take the furniture out of the house. Take the books out of the bookcase. The Explore Activity showed why this is so. When a force is applied, objects with less mass accelerate more quickly. An empty bookcase has less mass than a filled bookcase. Less force is needed to get an empty bookcase to move.

The experiment with the cart, books, and rubber bands shows how acceleration, mass, and force are related. Isaac Newton summarized the relationship in his *second law of motion*. This law says that the acceleration of an object is related to the object's mass and to the amount of force applied to the object. The law is written as

$F = ma$, or "the net force on an object equals the object's mass times the object's acceleration."

The net force is the combined effect of all the forces together. When you learned about the first law, you saw that a net force is needed to make an object accelerate. The second law says exactly how much a certain net force will make an object accelerate. Two results of Newton's second law are:

1. For a given net force, objects with a greater mass have less acceleration.

2. For objects of a given mass, a greater force results in a greater acceleration.

A rocket being launched

227

How Does Newton's Second Law Work?

DRAG

DRAG FORCE FROM AIR

ACCELERATION

DRAG FORCE FROM AIR

FRICTION

ACCELERATION

DRAG FORCE FROM AIR

FRICTION

What Happens to Weight in Space?

Did you ever hear or read that astronauts in orbiting satellites are "weightless"? Does weight disappear in space? Look at the photograph on this page.

The gravitational pull of Earth is quite large even several hundred kilometers from the surface. Satellites and the astronauts in them have weight as they orbit Earth. Why then do objects in the photograph float around as if they have no weight? Carry out the following Quick Lab for a clue.

Objects float around inside this orbiting space shuttle, making it seem as if they have no weight.

Free Fall

HYPOTHESIZE A water-filled plastic bottle has a small hole near the bottom. What happens to the water in the bottle? If the bottle were dropped and falling freely, what would happen to the water then? Write a hypothesis in your *Science Journal*.

MATERIALS

- water-filled plastic bottle with a small hole in the side near the bottom
- *Science Journal*

PROCEDURES

1. Put your finger over the hole in the water-filled plastic bottle. Then go outdoors.

2. **OBSERVE** Remove your finger from the hole for a second or two. Record in your *Science Journal* your observations of whether or not water comes out of the hole.

3. **OBSERVE** Now hold the bottle high and drop it, watching the hole. Does water continue to come out of the hole? Record your observations.

CONCLUDE AND APPLY

INFER How does the weight of the water make it behave when you hold the bottle? Did the water appear to have any weight when it was falling? Use your observations to support your answer.

235

What Is Weightlessness?

The Quick Lab showed that freely falling objects do not appear to have weight. To see why, imagine a parachutist standing in a plane on a weight scale. The scale would read the parachutist's normal weight. What if a trapdoor then opened, allowing the parachutist and the scale to begin falling freely? There would be nothing to keep the parachutist pressed onto the scale—the scale would no longer read any weight.

In fact anything else that fell through the trapdoor of the plane would fall alongside the parachutist and the scale, because all things fall at the same rate. The parachutist, the scale, and any other falling objects would appear to be floating with respect to one another. They would all have weight, but this weight could not be detected.

Like the parachutist and the scale, astronauts in an orbiting satellite are falling freely to Earth. Since everything in the spacecraft is falling together, the weight of any object cannot be detected.

To prepare for performing tasks in space, astronauts must practice in simulated weightless conditions. As the photograph shows, one method is to work underwater, because water reduces the weight of submerged objects. The other photograph shows astronauts flying in a jet that travels on a curved path. The result is a number of seconds of free fall, which feels just like the conditions in an orbiting spacecraft.

Satellites

Why does a satellite stay in orbit? Why doesn't it simply plunge to Earth like a bullet fired from a gun? The diagram on page 237 shows why this doesn't happen. An orbiting satellite moves rapidly sideways at the same time that it is falling toward the center of Earth. Both motions happen continuously, and they combine to keep the satellite on a curved path. Placing a satellite in orbit requires accelerating it to a sideways velocity great enough to keep its path of motion from colliding with the surface of Earth.

Astronauts in a jet aircraft

Astronauts underwater

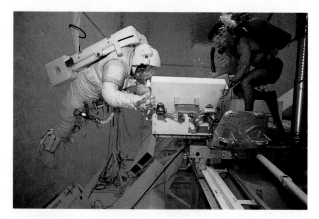

When a satellite or the space shuttle is launched into orbit, a large rocket propels it to a very large sideways velocity (red), perhaps as much as 28,000 km/h. Even though it is falling freely to Earth due to gravity (green), its sideways motion is just right to keep it on an oval or circular path (blue).

Newton's second and third laws, like the first law, help us to understand motion and forces. This helps engineers design and build everything from cars to aircraft to satellites. For example, a rocket must reach a velocity of about 11 km/s to escape the gravity of Earth and travel into deep space. Knowing this engineers can determine just how much force a rocket engine must develop to carry a rocket of a given mass into deep space. This knowledge aids them in designing rocket engines. In addition the force produced by existing rocket engines places a limit on how much mass a rocket can carry aloft. A knowledge of Newton's laws allows scientists to determine what this mass limit is.

REVIEW

1. A heavy truck and a light car have exactly the same motor. Which can accelerate faster? Why?

2. **PREDICT** What if you are standing on in-line skates and you toss a heavy ball forward? What will happen to you? Why?

3. One train car is at rest. Another identical car moves into it, going to the right at 2 m/s, and the two couple together. Both cars move off to the right at 1 m/s. Why do they move to the right? Why do they move at 1 m/s instead of 2 m/s?

4. What would happen to your mass if you traveled to Mars? Why?

5. **CRITICAL THINKING** *Analyze* What if you are in deep space, where a balance or spring scale will not work because there is no gravity? Describe another method you can use to compare the mass of objects.

WHY IT MATTERS THINK ABOUT IT
Imagine that your home somehow became like a satellite in free fall. How would the things you ordinarily do at home be different when everything acts like it is weightless?

WHY IT MATTERS WRITE ABOUT IT
Describe some examples of everyday activities at home that would be very different if you were in free fall. Be sure to explain how they would be different.

Riding the Winds

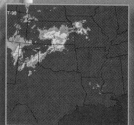   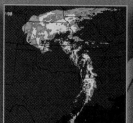 

Weather forecasters report that good or bad weather is "on the way." How do they know? What's pushing weather their way? Global winds!

These global winds are caused by the uneven heating of Earth. It creates areas of high and low pressure in the atmosphere, and wind forms when air moves from a high to a low.

Because the Sun's rays hit most directly near the equator, the warmest air is there. It has a low density above denser cold air moving in from the North and South Poles. Earth's rotation turns air north of the equator to the right and air south of the equator to the left. All this movement results in distinct wind patterns that influence our weather.

Between the equator and 30° latitude north or south are the trade winds. Once these winds blew the sails of giant trade ships from Europe to the New World. The northern trades can also bring storms from the Atlantic that become hurricanes before making landfall in the Caribbean or the southeastern United States.

The prevailing westerlies move U.S. weather systems from west to east.

Science, Technology, and Society

Between the 30° and 60° latitudes, winds blow in the opposite direction from the trade winds. These prevailing westerlies once pushed sailing ships back to Europe.

The polar easterlies blow to the southwest near the North Pole and to the northwest near the South Pole.

At higher altitudes narrow belts of strong winds—the jet stream—blow west to east. These winds average 100–185 kilometers per hour (60–111 miles per hour). Pilots often ride the jet stream for the fastest way home!

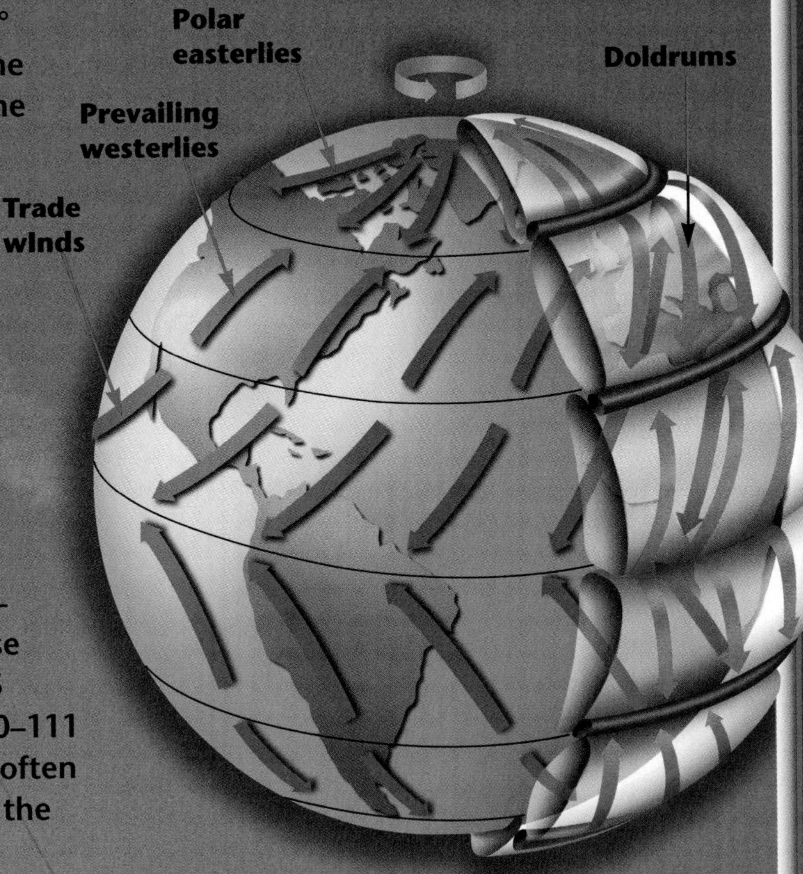

Polar easterlies

Doldrums

Prevailing westerlies

Trade winds

DISCUSSION STARTER

1. Why are there different types of global winds circling Earth?

2. The doldrums are a windless zone on the equator where the air seems motionless. Which direction is the air going? Why?

To learn more about global winds, visit *www.mhschool.com/science* and select the keyword GLOBAL.

inter**NET**
CONNECTION

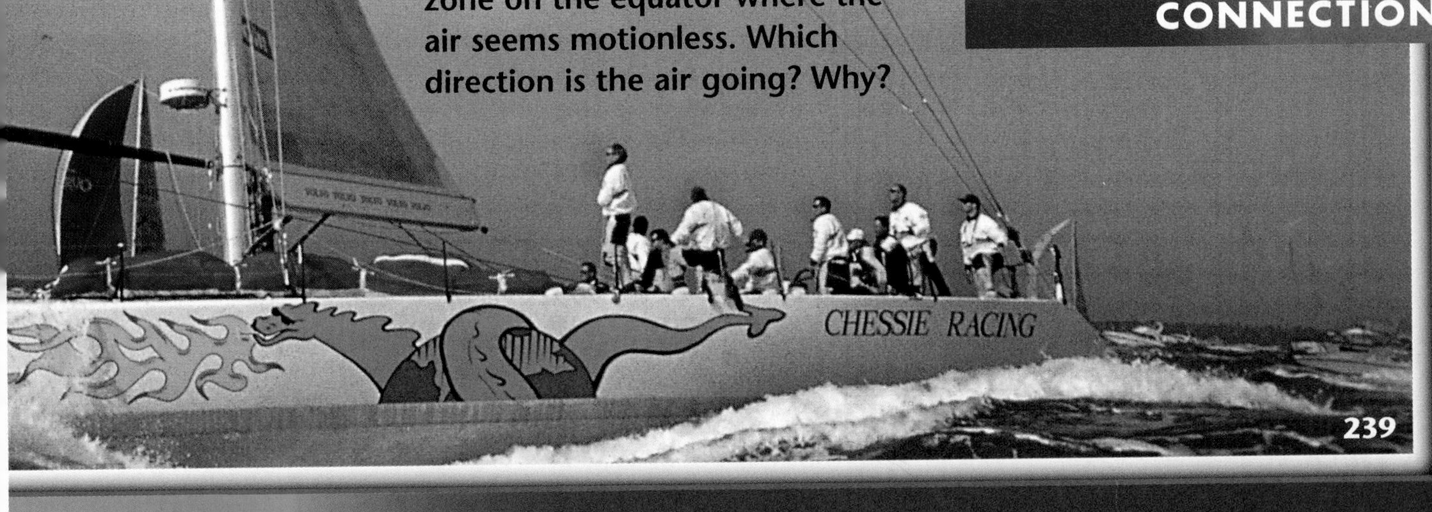

CHESSIE RACING

SCIENCE WORDS

acceleration p.202

average
  speed p.199

balanced
  forces p.216

force p.210

friction p.211

gravity p.214

inertia p.218

momentum p.232

position p.196

unbalanced
  forces p.217

velocity p.200

USING SCIENCE WORDS

Number a paper from 1 to 10. Fill in 1 to 5 with words from the list above.

1. To find the __?__ of something, divide the total distance traveled by the amount of time.

2. __?__ is the tendency of an object to oppose a change in motion.

3. When acting together on a single object, __?__ do not cancel each other out.

4. The location of an object is its __?__ .

5. The __?__ of an object is how fast and in what direction it is moving.

6–10. Pick five words from the list above that were not used in 1 to 5, and use each in a sentence.

UNDERSTANDING SCIENCE IDEAS

11. How can many pushes or pulls act on an object without causing it to speed up or slow down?

12. If you tie a rock to a string and swing it over your head, in what direction will it fly if the string breaks?

13. How can one value represent how fast an object travels even though its speed is changing?

14. What can you do to make a trunk go faster when you push it?

15. Why does a star move when it is orbited by a planet?

USING IDEAS AND SKILLS

16. **READING SKILL: FIND THE MAIN IDEA** Why do objects float around inside a spacecraft that is orbiting Earth even though they are not weightless?

17. Why would it be very difficult to walk on a tile floor if someone put a very slippery substance on your shoes?

18. Why is it wrong to show a spacecraft traveling at constant velocity with its rear engines blazing?

19. **PREDICT/USE NUMBERS** A train travels 24 m in 1 s, 48 m in 2 s, and 72 m in 3 s. What will its distance be at 4 s if it moves at a constant speed?

20. **THINKING LIKE A SCIENTIST** Why do car engineers carry out test crashes with model passengers? Why do they need to carry out many crashes?

PROBLEMS and PUZZLES

Roll Up Create an antigravity device! You'll need to tape two large funnels together at the wide ends. Form a gently sloping track using two yardsticks propped on top of two books of different heights. The yardsticks should be closer together on the lower end. Now place the funnels at the lower, narrower end. What happens?

CHAPTER 6
WORK AND MACHINES

Can you lift several tons of soil and rock with your finger? Yes—but not just with your finger. You need help from a machine. In this case, push a button or pull a handle, and get a machine to do the work for you.

In this chapter explore how machines make it easier to do work.

In this chapter look for details that support the main idea of what you are reading.

241

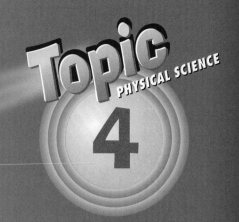

WHY IT MATTERS

Food gives us energy to do work.

SCIENCE WORDS

potential energy the energy stored in an object or material

gravitational potential energy the potential energy of an object located above the ground

kinetic energy the energy of a moving object

work force applied to an object times the distance the object moves

Energy and Work

Have you ever ridden a roller coaster at an amusement park? If so you know what happens on the way down a hill. How do roller coasters differ? Do you have any favorites?

One difference in roller coasters is the very first hill, the one you climb up s-l-o-w-l-y. Some of those first hills are much higher up than others. How does this difference change what happens on the way down?

EXPLORE

HYPOTHESIZE Does the speed of a roller coaster depend on how tall the hills are? If so which would give the faster ride— tall hills or lower hills? Write a hypothesis in your *Science Journal*. How would you test your ideas?

How Is Work Calculated when Objects Are Pushed or Pulled?

The students in the diagram are pushing a stalled car into a parking space. How much work is done if they push the car 8 meters? To calculate the work, we must know the applied force and the distance the car moves. The distance is 8 meters. As the diagram shows, each student applies a force of 300 newtons. Since there are two students, the total applied force must be 600 newtons. Now we can find the work:

Work = force x distance
Work = 600 newtons x 8 meters
Work = 4,800 joules

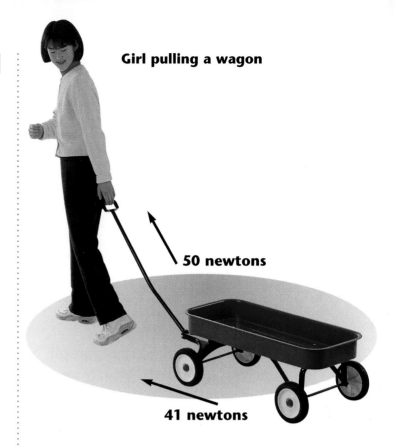

Girl pulling a wagon

50 newtons

41 newtons

Two students pushing a car

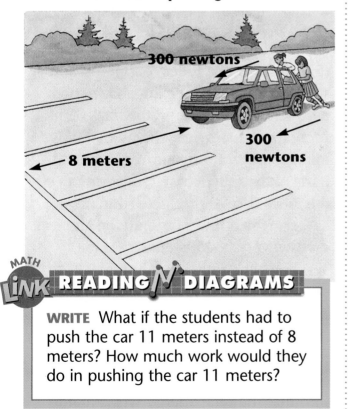

300 newtons

300 newtons

8 meters

MATH LINK READING DIAGRAMS

WRITE What if the students had to push the car 11 meters instead of 8 meters? How much work would they do in pushing the car 11 meters?

In the photograph the girl pulls a wagon a distance of 10 meters. Notice how the force she applies through the handle is 50 newtons. However, this is not the force that is acting in the direction that the wagon moves. As the photograph shows, only 41 newtons of the force acts in the direction that the wagon moves. The other 9 newtons of force pull up on the wagon and lighten its weight, but they do not act to move it forward.

To find the work the girl does, we must multiply the distance by the force that acts in the same direction as the motion. The distance is 10 meters and the force is 41 newtons. Now we can find the work:

Work = force x distance
Work = 41 newtons x 10 meters
Work = 410 joules

What kind of energy changes can you see in this photograph?

Can Energy Be Created or Destroyed?

The bicycle rider in the photograph stores energy in her body by eating foods. Then she changes this energy into kinetic energy by pedaling her bicycle to move it forward. As she rides across the countryside, she gains potential energy as she climbs hills. As she coasts down hills, her potential energy is changed back into kinetic energy, and she speeds up. When she stops, friction between the brake pads and the wheels slows the bike. The pads and the wheels get slightly warmer, and soon this heat escapes into the air.

The bicycle rider illustrates many changes of energy from one form to another. Yet, despite all of these changes, scientists believe that the total amount of energy in the universe remains constant. Energy may change in form, but it cannot be created or destroyed. The bicyclist cannot create energy—she must change some type of energy into the mechanical energy of the bike's turning pedals. Since she does not have a motor on her bike, she must use food energy stored in her body to turn the pedals.

The requirement that the total energy of the universe remain constant is called the law of conservation of energy. This law also applies to systems smaller than the universe as long as no energy is allowed to enter or leave the system.

For example, we might define a system to be a roller coaster and the surrounding air. At the top of the first hill, all of the roller coaster's energy is potential energy. As it accelerates down the first hill, its potential energy changes to kinetic energy. At the same time, though, the roller coaster loses some energy to air friction and friction between the wheels and the tracks. The friction produces heat energy that flows into the surrounding air from warmed parts of the roller coaster. In addition the roller coaster produces sound energy, which flows out into the air.

However, the total energy of the system of the roller coaster and surrounding air remains constant at all points during the ride. You would get the same answer for the total energy if you added up the amount of each form of energy at any instant. You would find that the total energy was equal to the potential energy the roller coaster had at the top of the first hill.

Why Conserve Energy?

Many nations of the world depend on coal, oil, and natural gas for sources of energy. These fuels may be used to produce electrical energy, or they may be burned in vehicles to produce mechanical energy. The worldwide demand for energy is becoming so great that a number of scientists fear that we will run dangerously short of coal, oil, and natural gas sometime in the 21st century.

We eat food to provide our bodies with energy, which is used to do work and to keep our body at 98°F. Dietary scientists must use a knowledge of energy and work to recommend proper diets for us to follow. They must know how much energy each food provides. They must also know how much energy various kinds of work consume. In a proper diet, the amount of food a person consumes must match the work done. If too much food is consumed, the person might gain unnecessary weight. If too little food is consumed, the person might lose weight and become weak.

A train carrying coal

REVIEW

1. Where would a book have more potential energy—on the floor or on top of a bookcase? Why?

2. **ANALYZE** Describe the energy changes that occur when a rubber ball falls and bounces to the floor.

3. A steel beam with a weight of 4,000 N is lifted 12 m by a crane. How much work is done?

4. A worker applies a 200-N force to a crate that he pushes 10 m across a floor. How much work does he do?

5. **CRITICAL THINKING** *Analyze* What if you lift a box from the floor to a height of 0.75 m? Then you carry it 4 m over to a 0.75-m-high table and place it there. Did carrying the box over to the table add to the amount of work done? Why?

WHY IT MATTERS THINK ABOUT IT
It takes work to launch a rocket into space. Think about the properties a rocket fuel would need if it were to be the best possible fuel for the job.

WHY IT MATTERS WRITE ABOUT IT
Write out a description of your ideal rocket fuel. Explain how it would be the best fuel for doing the work of launching a rocket.

READING SKILL
On page 250 what are some details that support the main idea that work = force x distance?

Can Car Crashes Be Safer?

Why are so many people injured in car crashes? One reason is that an impact can crush anyone in the car.

A moving car has kinetic energy. When it stops after hitting another car or a wall, its kinetic energy is converted into other forms of energy. Some goes into sound energy, so you hear a crash. Some becomes thermal energy, raising the temperatures of the objects involved. Some is used to crush or break the colliding objects.

How much will be crushed? It depends on the number of objects involved, what they're made of, and how fast they were moving when they hit. If two identical cars, moving at the same speed, hit head on, the kinetic energy is divided equally between them. They'll be equally crushed. However, if a car hits a solid concrete wall that doesn't crush easily, most of the kinetic energy goes into damaging the car.

96 FD 03

Crash tests determine how much damage will be done to a car and its occupants.

Science, Technology, and Society

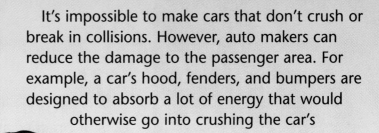

It's impossible to make cars that don't crush or break in collisions. However, auto makers can reduce the damage to the passenger area. For example, a car's hood, fenders, and bumpers are designed to absorb a lot of energy that would otherwise go into crushing the car's occupants. Auto engineers also try to design the car's frame so that if it collapses, it'll push the engine and other parts out away from people inside the car.

As long as people drive cars, there'll be crashes. However, auto engineers are using their knowledge of physics to help make cars as safe as possible!

DISCUSSION STARTER

1. Early cars had heavy steel bodies and rigid frames, but they didn't cause as much damage to passengers as newer cars do. What single factor makes the difference?

2. What's another danger that a collision may pose to the occupants of the cars?

96 F D 08

To learn more about the physics of car crashes, visit *www.mhschool.com/science* and select the keyword CRASH!

*inter***NET**
CONNECTION

WHY IT MATTERS

Simple machines make our lives easier.

SCIENCE WORDS

simple machine a device with few parts that makes it easier to do work

effort force the force applied to a machine

resistance force the force that a machine acts against

lever a simple machine made of a rigid bar on a pivot point

fulcrum the pivot point of a lever

mechanical advantage the number of times a machine multiplies the force applied

pulley a grooved wheel that turns by the action of a rope in the groove

wheel and axle a simple machine made of a handle or axis attached to the center of a wheel

How Levers Work

What does it take to win a rowboat race? Lots of practice and teamwork are two answers. Each rower must pull on the oars with as much force as possible.

Why are oars used instead of paddles? Why is more of the oar over the side of the boat than on the inside? Do you think it matters where you hold the oar?

Do you know what a seesaw is? Have you ever used a crowbar? Have you ever seen a car with a flat tire jacked up? Do you use your bare hands for cracking nuts? Why do scissors cut paper? How does a bat hit a home run?

EXPLORE

HYPOTHESIZE What determines how much force it takes to use an oar or any of the other levers? Write a hypothesis in your *Science Journal*. How would you test your idea?

EXPLORE ACTIVITY

Investigate How Machines Affect Force

Use a meterstick as a model to explore if the amount of force needed depends on where the force is applied.

PROCEDURES

1. Use the spring scale to measure the force it takes to lift the washers.

2. One partner ties and holds the string to the meterstick as shown.

3. Use the large paper clip to hang the washers from the meterstick about 20 cm away from the string. At the other end of the meterstick attach the spring scale about 20 cm away from the balance point. Measure how much force it takes to raise the weights. Record your results in your *Science Journal.*

4. **PREDICT** What will happen to the force if you move the spring scale so that it is 30 cm away from the balance point? Make a prediction, and try it.

5. **EXPERIMENT** Repeat this process with the spring scale at 40 cm away.

CONCLUDE AND APPLY

1. **OBSERVE** Which direction did you pull on the stick? Which direction did the weights move?

2. **EVALUATE** Was the force you exerted ever equal to the force exerted by the weight of the washers?

3. **OBSERVE** What happened as you moved the spring scale farther away from the balance point?

GOING FURTHER: Problem Solving

4. **ANALYZE** In order to lift the weights 15 cm, how far do you have to pull down on the spring scale? Does it matter if the spring scale is 20, 30, or 40 cm away from the balance point? Experiment to find out.

MATERIALS

- spring scale
- meterstick
- short piece of string
- large washers (or any object that can be used as a weight)
- large paper clip (to attach the weight to the meterstick)
- *Science Journal*

Hammer being used to pull a nail

How Do Machines Affect Force?

A machine is simply a device that makes it easier for us to do work. You should recall that in order to do work, we must apply a force to something and move it through a distance. The meterstick in the Explore Activity was used as a machine. The Explore Activity showed that a machine can change the amount of force needed to do work.

Machines can range from very basic—the hammer in the photograph—to very complex. The most basic kinds are called **simple machines**. These machines have few, if any, moving parts. The hammer is an example of a simple machine. When many simple machines are combined, a complex machine results.

Sometimes a simple machine merely changes the direction of a force we apply to something. This is an important way that a simple machine can make it more convenient to apply a force. Look at the hammer being used in the photograph. The force being applied to the handle by the person's hand is sideways. The force being applied to the nail by the hammer, though, is upward.

Machines can also increase the strength of an applied force. Imagine pulling the nail out of the board with your bare hands! The hammer makes the job much easier. Measurements show that the upward force applied by the hammer to the nail is greater than the downward force applied by the person's hand to the hammer handle.

The force that you apply to a simple machine is called the **effort force** (EF). The force against which the machine acts—like the resistance of the nail to being pulled in the photograph—is called the **resistance force** (RF). The force the machine applies to an object in response to our effort force is called the *output force*.

Machines usually help us by doing physical work. However, in the 1800s Charles Babbage, a mathematician and inventor, designed machines that did math calculations. These machines were computers, but they were mechanical rather than electrical. What advantage, if any, do you think an electrical computer has over a mechanical computer?

What Are Other Examples?

Here are two other devices based on a wheel and axle. The screwdriver's handle is the wheel, and its shaft is the axle. The screwdriver is able to multiply the effort applied to the handle. This makes it easier to turn screws in or out of wood or metal.

The pedals of the bicycle act as a wheel, and the sprocket to which they are attached is like an axle. Riders use the large sprocket for high-speed riding and the smaller sprockets for low-speed riding.

Screwdriver and screws

It would be very difficult to live in a world without machines. If your bare hands were the only tools you had, think how hard life would be! Thankfully we have simple machines like hammers, screwdrivers, and cranks to make tasks easier. In addition complex machines like cars—which we depend on heavily—are made from a combination of simple machines. Understanding simple machines helps us to design even better complex machines.

Pedals and sprockets on a bike

REVIEW

1. Which pries the lid off a paint can more easily—a long screwdriver or a short screwdriver? Why?

2. What if you want a first-class lever with a mechanical advantage that is less than 1? Where do you place the fulcrum? Why?

3. Your aunt wants to put a pulley in her garage to lift the top of her jeep upward from the side. Which is better—a single movable pulley or a single fixed pulley? Sketch how to place the pulley.

4. **DEFINE** What is a wheel and axle? Is a doorknob an example?

5. **CRITICAL THINKING** *Analyze* Design a pulley system that has a mechanical advantage of 6. Sketch your system.

WHY IT MATTERS THINK ABOUT IT
What if someone took all the tools in your home away for a day? Think about all of the jobs that would be impossible without them.

WHY IT MATTERS WRITE ABOUT IT
Write out a list of household tasks that you could not do without tools. For each one explain how the tool makes the task easier.

So Simple a Monkey Can Use It!

Which simple machine do both humans and chimps use? It's the lever! Chimps use sticks to lift rocks in search of food. Humans use iron bars to lift heavy rocks out of the way.

A wrench is a lever, too. One end fits an object that can be turned. The other end is the handle. The fulcrum is where the wrench holds the object.

Plumbers often use wrenches with very long handles to remove stuck pipe fittings. Why can wrenches turn the fittings easily when plumbers can't do it with bare hands? The longer the lever, the greater the mechanical advantage.

Complex machines have two or more simple machines. For example, pliers are just two levers attached at their fulcrums. So are scissors.

The fulcrum of a crane is where it attaches to a powerful engine. A pulley is used to lift the crane, and another pulley lifts heavy objects.

Why do you think they call it a monkey wrench?

Social Studies Link

A wheel and axle is a lever that changes a weak force moving in a large circle into a strong force moving in a smaller circle. This doesn't increase speed, because one rotation of the wheel always produces one rotation of the axle. Speed can be increased by connecting one wheel and axle to another of a different size, so that by turning one, you turn the other.

Gears are complex machines that have connected wheels with teeth to keep them from slipping. Almost any machine that has circular motion, from a bike to a food processor, uses gears to increase its speed or force.

DISCUSSION STARTER

1. Where on a bike would you find a complex machine of two levers?

2. Describe the simple machines that are combined in a wheelbarrow.

To learn more about simple machines, visit *www.mhschool.com/science* and select the keyword MONKEY!

inter**NET**
CONNECTION

WHY IT MATTERS

You need to understand simple machines to design complex machines.

SCIENCE WORDS

inclined plane a straight, slanted surface that is not moved when it is used

screw an inclined plane wrapped around a central bar

wedge one or a combination of two inclined planes that is moved when used

compound machine a combination of two or more machines

efficiency a ratio of the work done by a machine compared with the work put into the machine

How Inclined Planes Work

Have you ever ridden a bicycle up a steep hill? Why was it so hard to pedal?

Why are mountain roads long and winding? Would life be easier if we didn't have stairs to climb?

Why does the ramp in the picture have two parts? Why didn't they build just one short ramp? Have you ever seen a wedge used to split a log? Why can a wedge do this?

EXPLORE

HYPOTHESIZE Does the slant of a ramp change the force you need to use the ramp? Do steeper ramps require you to use a greater force? A smaller force? Write a hypothesis in your *Science Journal*. How would you test your ideas?

Where Do We Go from Here?

Have you seen the many wonders of space that space probes and astronauts have discovered? The table below lists just some of the many space missions planned for the beginning of the next millennium.

Much of astronomy has no practical use. However, many people want to learn about it because of their curiosity. They want to know what this universe is made out of, where it came from, and where it's going.

A practical use of astronomy is that knowing the position of the stars helps navigators.

FUTURE SPACE MISSIONS

Year	Country	Spacecraft	Carrying Crew?	Mission
2001	U.S.A.	*Pluto Express*	No	Study Pluto and Charon
2002	U.S.A.	*Columbia*	Yes	Hubble service flight
2003	U.S.A.	*Rosetta*	No	Land on comet Wirtanen
2005	U.S.A.	*Mars Surveyor*	No	Return Martian soil samples to Earth

REVIEW

1. Why do you think people become astronomers?

2. What is meant by light? Is all light visible? Explain.

3. **COMPARE AND CONTRAST** What is the difference between a reflecting telescope and a refracting telescope? How are they alike?

4. What is needed for people to travel in space vehicles?

5. **CRITICAL THINKING** *Analyze* What are the advantages of space travel over using telescopes to explore the universe? What have we learned this way? What are some disadvantages of space travel?

WHY IT MATTERS THINK ABOUT IT
When you look at the stars at night, what questions come to mind? What things about the universe are you most curious about?

WHY IT MATTERS WRITE ABOUT IT
Write your questions down. Plan how you might find the answers. It could be by asking someone or looking in a book. It could also be by discovering the answers yourself.

Free FALLING

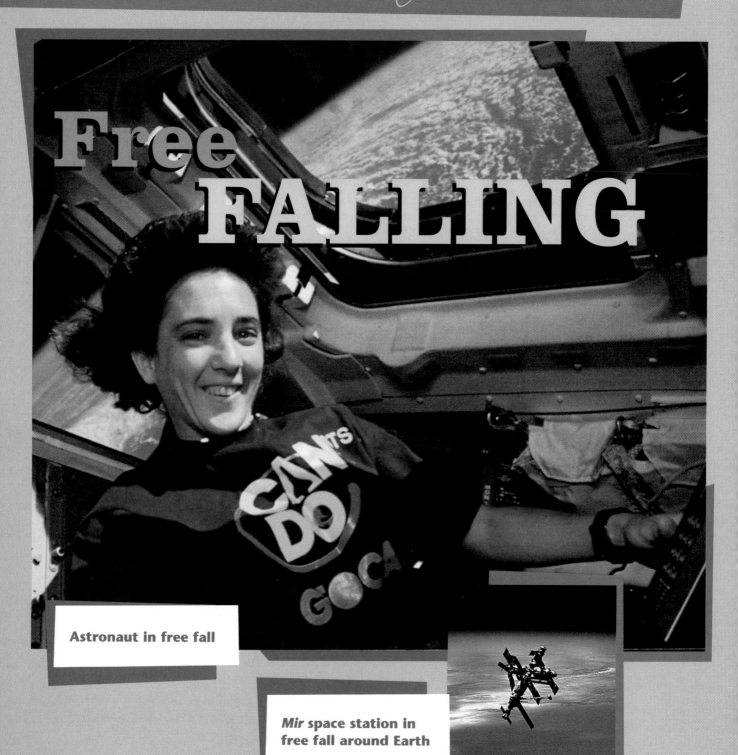

Astronaut in free fall

Mir space station in free fall around Earth

Would you be weightless in space? No, you would be in free fall, something Isaac Newton wrote about 300 years ago!

According to Newton a cannonball shot off parallel to the ground would orbit Earth. Two forces would create this orbit—the force pushing the cannonball forward and gravity. If the force launching the cannonball were great enough, gravity would pull the cannonball into orbit around Earth.

The same principle keeps the space shuttle and *Mir* space station in orbit. They are launched with enough power to keep them traveling forward, and the pull of gravity keeps them in free fall around Earth.

The astronauts inside the spacecraft are in free fall, too. They train for the experience at the Weightless Environment Training Facility (WET-F), a swimming pool that simulates working conditions in space. Astronauts wear weights so they have the same buoyancy as the water. However, in the pool, unlike space, the astronauts can push against the water and swim.

Because of the lack of gravity in free fall, astronauts can lose calcium and bone density. Their muscles weaken, and astronauts look about an inch taller because their spines aren't being pulled down.

Astronauts re-create free fall in WET-F training.

Discussion
Starter

Explain why astronauts feel "weightless" in space.

WHY IT MATTERS

The Sun makes daytime and the seasons possible, but only because Earth is moving.

SCIENCE WORDS

rotation a complete spin on an axis

International Date Line the 180° line of longitude

standard time zone a belt 15° wide in longitude in which all places have the same time

revolution one complete trip around the Sun

Earth and the Sun

Where does your shadow point as you enter school each day? Where does it point as you leave? Why is there a difference?

What does this shadow tell you? Where is the Sun located with respect to what you see in the photograph? What time of day is it? What evidence supports your inference? If you took a picture of the shadow every hour, how would it change as the day goes on?

EXPLORE

HYPOTHESIS In what direction does the Sun rise? Set? At what time of the day is the Sun highest above the horizon? How high above the horizon will the Sun get today? Write a hypothesis in your *Science Journal*. Test your ideas without looking at the Sun.

Life Science Link

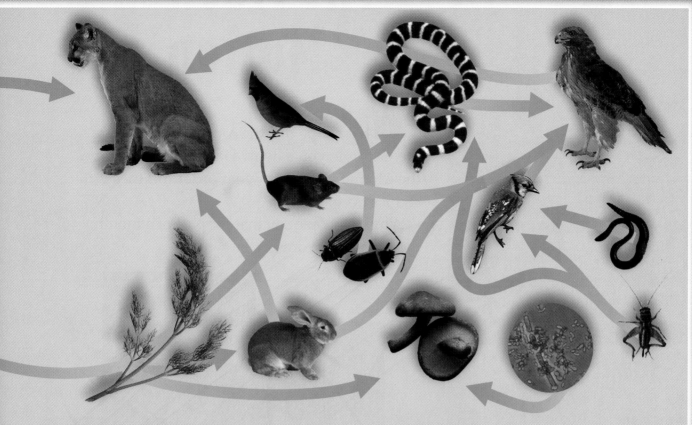

A complex food web assures that if one species dies out, another can take its place in the food chain. For example, what if a virus kills off all the rabbits in our sample chain. The snakes will become extinct, too, if rabbits are the only food they eat. The eagles will also die off, if they depend solely on snakes for food. However, if the chain is part of a rich and varied food web, the flow of energy can remain unbroken.

Only about ten percent of the energy is transferred between each level from producers to tertiary consumers.

Why? Each organism uses energy while working and doesn't completely digest all the food it eats. Picture this process as an energy pyramid, with plants at the bottom and animals that eat other animals, such as lions and humans, at the top. To get all the energy they need to survive, the top dogs are dependent on all the organisms below them.

DISCUSSION STARTER

1. Explain the flow of energy in a food chain.

2. Why is a food web more stable than a food chain?

To learn more about the food chain, visit *www.mhschool.com/science* and select the keyword LINKS.

*inter*NET CONNECTION

317

WHY IT MATTERS

Watch the Moon over a month and you'll find some interesting patterns.

SCIENCE WORDS

phase of the Moon the shape of the lighted part of the Moon seen from Earth at any time

lunar eclipse a blocking of a view of the full Moon when the Moon passes into Earth's shadow

solar eclipse a blocking out of a view of the Sun when Earth passes through the Moon's shadow

tide the regular rise and fall of the water level along a shoreline

The Moon in Motion

What shape did the Moon seem to have the last time you saw it? Describe other shapes the Moon has had. In what order did these shapes occur?

Why do people say that for part of a month, the Moon is waxing, or growing?

EXPLORE

HYPOTHESIZE Why does the Moon seem to change shape? Is Earth casting a shadow on it? Do the shapes result from the positions of the Moon, Earth, and the Sun? Write a hypothesis in your *Science Journal.* Test your ideas.

Investigate Why the Moon Changes Its Appearance

Use a model to explore how a ball can appear to change shape.

MATERIALS

- 3 balls (one for Earth, one for the Sun, one for the Moon)
- black tape
- crayon or felt-tipped pen (to label each ball)
- *Science Journal*

PROCEDURES

1. **MAKE A MODEL** The Sun, Earth, and the Moon are each represented by a ball. The half-dark/half-light ball represents the Moon. The light side always faces the Sun. The dark side always faces away from it.

2. **MAKE A MODEL** Arrange your model of Earth, the Sun, and the Moon so that someone on Earth would see the lighted portion of the Moon as a circle, as shown on page 318. Remember to keep the lighted side of the ball facing the Sun.

3. **COMMUNICATE** Draw a diagram in your *Science Journal* to show the location of Earth, the Sun, and the Moon in your model. Show where Earth's shadow falls.

4. **EXPERIMENT** Move the Moon around Earth in the model system so that you can match the other pictures on page 318.

CONCLUDE AND APPLY

1. **OBSERVE** How are Earth, the Sun, and the Moon arranged in order to see the views of the Moon on page 318?

2. **DRAW CONCLUSIONS** Do you think the monthly cycle of light and dark on the Moon is caused by Earth's shadow on the Moon? Explain your answer.

GOING FURTHER: Problem Solving

3. **ANALYZE** In which direction must the Moon move around Earth to produce the shapes in the proper order?

Why Does the Moon Change Its Appearance?

How can we summarize the motion of Earth and the Moon? The Moon revolves around Earth and Earth revolves around the Sun. You also know that the Moon changes its appearance in monthly cycles. The amount of the bright part of the Moon changes shape. The **phase of the Moon** is the shape of the lighted part of the Moon at any given time. What causes these shapes? The Explore Activity provided a model to help answer this question.

Remember, half of the Moon is always lighted by the Sun. However, you can't always see all of that half. Sometimes you can see only small amounts of this portion of the Moon. Sometimes you can see a lot. Sometimes you can't see any of the lighted half of the Moon at all!

The phase, or shape, of the Moon that you see depends on the position of the Sun, the Moon, and Earth with respect to each other.

- *New Moon* **Phase:** At New Moon the Moon is between Earth and the Sun. The half of the Moon lit by the Sun is opposite the half that faces Earth. As a result, you cannot see any of the Moon's sunlit half.

- **Waxing Phases:** As the Moon orbits Earth, more of its sunlit half becomes visible. When half of the sunlit side is visible, the Moon is at *First Quarter phase*. As you see it, the right half of the Moon is visible. If all of its sunlit half is visible, the Moon is at the phase called *Second Quarter*, or the *Full Moon*.

   When the phase that is visible is more than New Moon but less than First Quarter, the phase is called a *Waxing Crescent*. *Waxing* means "growing larger." When the phase visible is more than First Quarter but less than Full Moon, the phase is a *Waxing Gibbous* Moon.

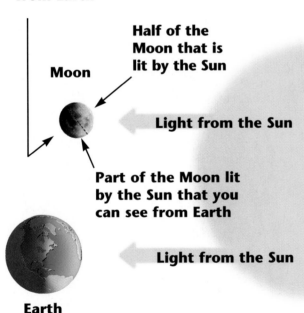

Half of the Moon visible from Earth

Half of the Moon that is lit by the Sun

Moon

Light from the Sun

Part of the Moon lit by the Sun that you can see from Earth

Light from the Sun

Earth

Note the positions of the Sun, the Moon, and Earth during the Waxing Crescent phase.

- **Waning Phases:** After Full Moon the part of the sunlit half of the Moon you can see gets smaller. The phases you see are the same as from new to full, only in reverse.

When the left half of the Moon is visible, the phase of the Moon is the *Third Quarter*, or *Last Quarter*. The phase of the Moon that is less than Full Moon phase but more than Third Quarter is called a *Waning Gibbous* Moon. *Waning* means "growing smaller." When the phase you see is less than Third Quarter but more than New Moon, the phase is called a *Waning Crescent*.

PHASES OF THE MOON

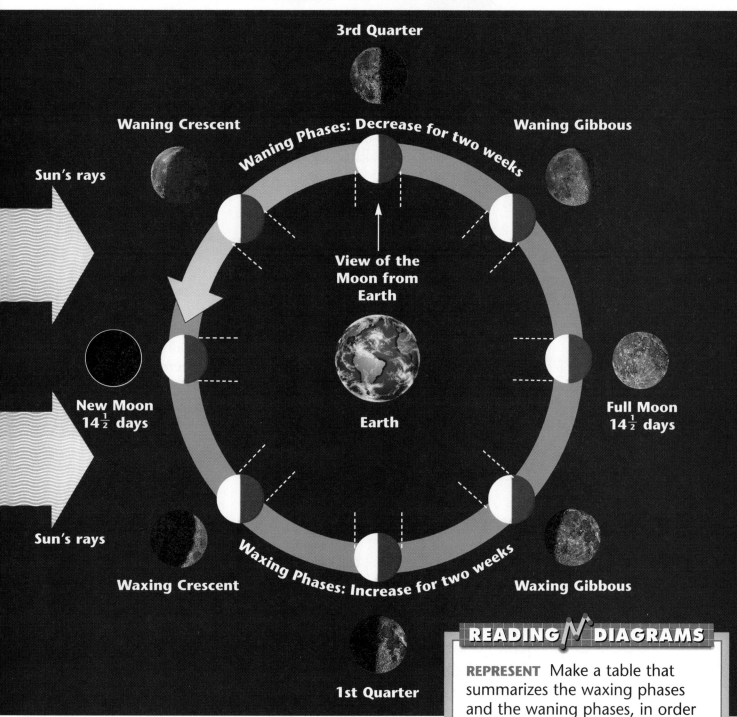

3rd Quarter

Waning Crescent

Waning Phases: Decrease for two weeks

Waning Gibbous

Sun's rays

View of the Moon from Earth

New Moon 14½ days

Earth

Full Moon 14½ days

Sun's rays

Waxing Crescent

Waxing Phases: Increase for two weeks

Waxing Gibbous

1st Quarter

READING DIAGRAMS

REPRESENT Make a table that summarizes the waxing phases and the waning phases, in order from New Moon to New Moon.

LUNAR ECLIPSE

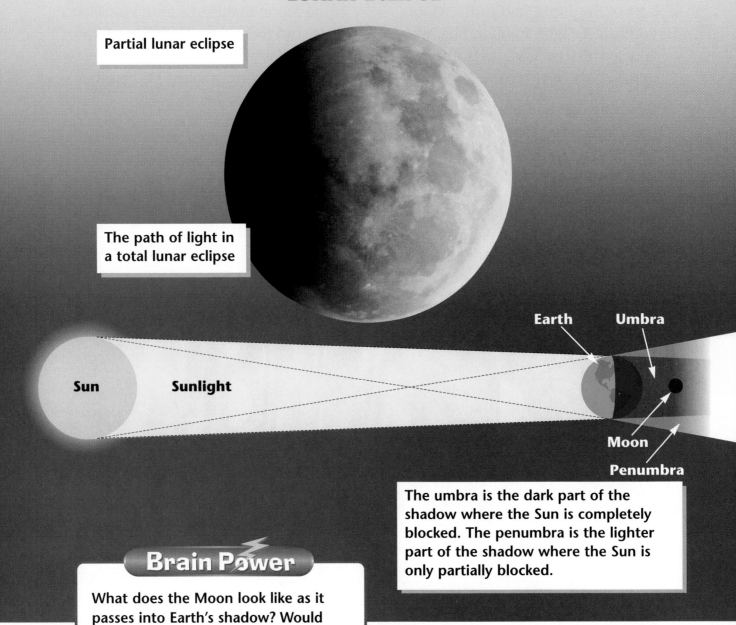

Partial lunar eclipse

The path of light in a total lunar eclipse

Earth Umbra

Sun Sunlight

Moon

Penumbra

The umbra is the dark part of the shadow where the Sun is completely blocked. The penumbra is the lighter part of the shadow where the Sun is only partially blocked.

Brain Power

What does the Moon look like as it passes into Earth's shadow? Would you see phases of the Moon? Explain.

Can Earth's Shadow Hide the Moon?

Recall that the Moon revolves around Earth. Recall also that at the same time, Earth revolves around the Sun.

The plane of the Moon's orbit is tilted to the plane of Earth's orbit around the Sun. As a result the Moon is usually above or below Earth's orbit. Twice a month the Moon crosses the plane of Earth's orbit. When this takes place at full Moon, the Moon might pass through Earth's shadow. When this happens a **lunar eclipse** occurs. Our view of the full Moon is blocked.

What Is an Eclipse of the Sun?

When Earth passes through the Moon's shadow, a solar eclipse occurs. At what phase must a **solar eclipse** occur?

For a solar eclipse to occur, the Moon must be in a straight line between the Sun and Earth. This arrangement happens at New Moon phase. A solar eclipse can occur when the Moon crosses the plane of Earth's orbit at New Moon phase.

Have you ever seen a total solar eclipse? It is a fascinating sight. At the greatest part of the eclipse, the Moon completely hides the Sun. All you can see is the gases in the outer atmosphere surrounding the Sun.

Earth-orbiting satellites have actually been able to photograph an eclipse! See the picture below. Where do you think the eclipse of the Sun is occurring at this moment?

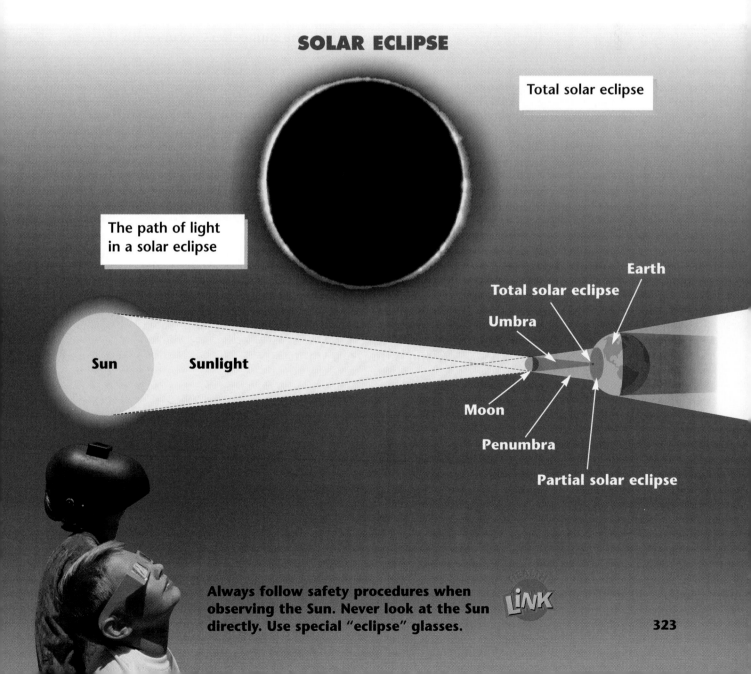

SOLAR ECLIPSE

Total solar eclipse

The path of light in a solar eclipse

Sun

Sunlight

Earth

Total solar eclipse

Umbra

Moon

Penumbra

Partial solar eclipse

Always follow safety procedures when observing the Sun. Never look at the Sun directly. Use special "eclipse" glasses.

LINK

What Are Tides?

Have you ever been at the seashore and watched the ocean waves? If you have, you may have noticed that as time passed the waves came higher up on the shore. You were looking at the **tide** coming in. Tides are the regular rise and fall of the water level along a shore.

The tides are caused by the pull of the Moon's gravity on Earth. The Moon's gravity is stonger on the side of Earth that is facing the Moon. This causes the water to bulge on this side of Earth. A bulge also forms on the side facing away from the Moon.

At certain times of the year, the alignment of the Sun, the Moon, and Earth causes what are called *spring tides* and *neap tides*.

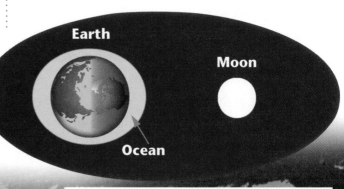

These tides are caused by the Moon. The same effect occurs with the Sun.

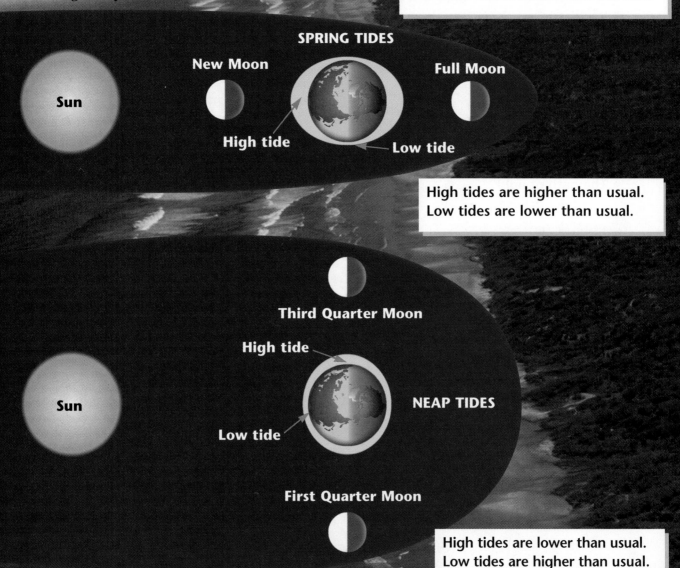

SPRING TIDES

New Moon

Full Moon

Sun

High tide

Low tide

High tides are higher than usual. Low tides are lower than usual.

Third Quarter Moon

High tide

Sun

NEAP TIDES

Low tide

First Quarter Moon

High tides are lower than usual. Low tides are higher than usual.

Skill: Making a Model

MODEL OF THE TIDES

Now that you have read about spring and neap tides, you and a partner are going to practice making a model of a spring tide. How good a model can you make?

PROCEDURES

1. MAKE A MODEL How are you going to arrange the materials to model a spring tide? A neap tide? How are you going to model the pull on Earth due to the Moon and the Sun? Talk with your partner. Record your ideas in your *Science Journal.*

2. EXPERIMENT Test your model. Repeat your test, switching roles with your partner.

3. COMMUNICATE In your *Science Journal*, sketch your model. Write or draw the results of your test.

CONCLUDE AND APPLY

1. OBSERVE How did you model the pull of the Moon and the Sun on Earth? What results did you obtain?

2. ANALYZE How well did your model work? What went right with your model? What things did you have difficulty with in your model?

3. COMPARE AND CONTRAST Share your model and your results with your classmates. Did other teams have similar successes or difficulties? How would you change your model to make it work better?

What Does the Moon's Surface Look Like?

HISTORY LINK

When you look at the Moon from Earth, it shows features that can be easily seen. When the *Apollo* astronauts visited the Moon in the 1960s and 1970s, they took close-up pictures of many of these same features. Some of the features looked the same way they looked from Earth. Some of them looked very different. What do we know about these features?

- **Craters** were formed by the impact of objects from space. Craters are in many sizes and shapes. Some have peaks in the center. Some craters also seem to have rings that make them look like bull's-eye targets. When the meteorites hit the surface, the impact sent out waves, just like when you throw a rock into a pond. The waves formed rings, or rims, around the craters. Even though the Moon and Earth are hit by space objects at about the same rate, there are more craters on the Moon. This is because erosion on Earth wears away Earth craters. There is no erosion on the Moon.

- **Maria** (singular, *mare*) are large, dark, flat areas. They were the "seas" seen by the people of long ago. You can still see them if you look now. However, the maria are not really seas. They were formed by huge lava flows that covered low-lying areas, including the craters, billions of years ago.

- **Highlands** are light-colored, heavily cratered regions at higher elevations than maria.

- **Mountains** are named after mountain ranges on Earth. These features were formed as a result of violent impacts of debris from space that created the maria.

- **Valleys** are cigar-shaped depressions. The most famous is the Alpine Valley. It is located in the mountain range known as the Alps. The Alpine Valley is on the northeastern edge of Mare Imbrium.

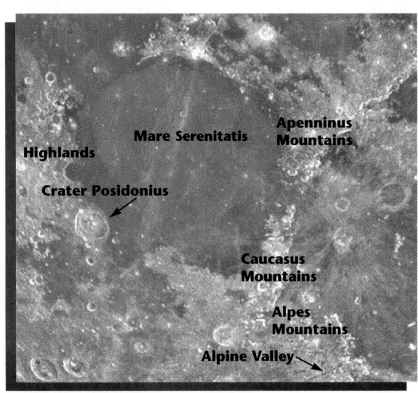

Highlands

Mare Serenitatis

Apenninus Mountains

Crater Posidonius

Caucasus Mountains

Alpes Mountains

Alpine Valley

Various features of the moon's surface as observed from Ringgold, Georgia.

What Have We Learned About the Moon?

The *Apollo* missions to the Moon have given us much data about the Moon. We have also learned a lot from telescopes and probes sent to the Moon.

What Was Learned

- The Moon has no magnetic field today. However, it had a weak one in the past.

- Seismometers show that the Moon is still being hit by meteors.

- Heat-flow experiments show that the Moon is losing heat.

- Rock samples brought back to Earth have provided clues to the early history of the Earth and Moon system.

Apollo **changed our ideas about the Moon.**

Human beings get great satisfaction when a simple idea can explain many different observations. We can take pleasure then in the simple idea of this lesson. The Moon moves around Earth as Earth goes around the Sun. This simple model explains Moon phases, eclipses, and tides.

REVIEW

1. Why do we see the phases of the Moon?

2. How is a lunar eclipse different from a solar eclipse?

3. **MAKE A MODEL** Where are the Sun, the Moon, and Earth during a neap tide? During a spring tide?

4. How does the Moon's surface compare with Earth's?

5. **CRITICAL THINKING** *Apply* During a total lunar eclipse, the Moon looks completely dark as seen from Earth. When this happens what do you think Earth looks like from the Moon? To answer this draw a model of a lunar eclipse.

WHY IT MATTERS THINK ABOUT IT
What if you receive an E-mail message from your friend? Your friend writes that the phases of the Moon are caused by Earth's shadow cast on the Moon. Why is this not correct?

WHY IT MATTERS WRITE ABOUT IT
Write a reply to your friend that explains why Moon phases cannot be caused by shadows. Then give the correct explanation.

Straddling Worlds

Imagine living in a place where waves continually pound you, a place that is dry one minute and submerged the next. That's what it's like for the creatures of the tidal zone. Within each distinct area, animals and plants make the most of what's available.

THE LOW-TIDE ZONE
Sea urchins dig holes in the rocks to assure that even at low tide, water will fill their homes. Sea urchins graze on algae. They scrape algae off surfaces with teeth around their mouth.

THE MIDTIDE ZONE
The spiny starfish, or sea star, uses its suction-cup feet to stay put even when the waves are rough. To eat, this critter sticks its feet to either side of a mussel shell, pries it open, inserts its own stomach, and digests the mussel!

Life Science Link

THE HIGH-TIDE ZONE

The barnacle has a hard shell to bear the crushing weight of pounding surf. It also has a gluey substance on its head. It sticks to rocks so it won't wash away. To eat, a barnacle kicks its featherlike feet into the water and moves plankton into its shell.

THE SPLASH ZONE

Animals in the splash zone don't need much moisture. Periwinkle snails scrape algae off splash-zone rocks with their sharp tongues. However, a dogwinkle snail can drill through a periwinkle's shell and eat the animal inside!

DISCUSSION STARTER

1. What makes life difficult for animals and plants in the tidal zone?

2. How have animals adapted to life in the tidal zone?

To learn more about life in the tidal zones, visit *www.mhschool.com/science* and select the keyword TIDES.

*inter*NET
CONNECTION

SCIENCE WORDS

frequency p. 295   rotation p. 308

lunar eclipse p. 322   solar eclipse p. 323

reflection p. 294   telescope p. 293

refraction p. 294   tide p. 324

revolution p. 312   universe p. 292

USING SCIENCE WORDS

Number a paper from 1 to 10. Fill in 1 to 5 with words from the list above.

1. When the Moon blocks our view of the Sun, it is called a __?__.

2. The regular rise and fall of the water level along a shore is called the __?__.

3. The bending of waves when they go from one substance to another is called __?__.

4. Earth makes one __?__ each year.

5. __?__ is the bouncing of waves off a surface.

6–10. Pick five words from the list above that were not used in 1 to 5, and use each in a sentence.

UNDERSTANDING SCIENCE IDEAS

11. What properties distinguish radio waves from visible light?

12. Telescopes can be designed based on which two properties of light?

13. The flattening of Earth at the poles and the bulging at the equator is evidence for what?

14. Describe what astronomers study.

15. What can make the Moon look completely dark as seen from Earth?

USING IDEAS AND SKILLS

16. **READING SKILL: CAUSE AND EFFECT** How do astronomers find out about the universe if they cannot leave Earth?

17. Is the cycle of seasons due to a change in the tilt of Earth's axis?

18. Why are there more craters on the Moon than on Earth?

19. **MAKE A MODEL** How does the arrangement of Earth, the Sun, and the Moon affect the tides on Earth?

20. **THINKING LIKE A SCIENTIST** The force of gravity depends on your distance from Earth's center. How would you test this hypothesis?

PROBLEMS and PUZZLES

Lunar Month For one month observe the Moon at the same time of the day. Draw its shape, and label it with the date and time you observed it. Label the drawings with the phases you observe. Is the Moon always in the same part of the sky? How did the Moon's shape change from day to day?

CHAPTER 8

THE SOLAR SYSTEM AND BEYOND

When you think of a cloud, what comes to mind? A storm? A sunny day? How about a nursery?

This is a kind of cloud in outer space. In a way it is a nursery. In this cloud stars will eventually be born. Revolving around some of these stars might even be planets!

In this chapter you will compare and contrast many things. To *compare* means to tell how things are alike. To *contrast* means to tell how things are different.

The Inner Solar System

How are planets and stars different? On clear nights, away from city lights, stars appear to be points of light. However, some of these points of light are not stars. Some are planets—such as Jupiter and Venus. How can you tell them from stars?

The arrows in these pictures point to a planet at two different times of the year. What has changed between the two pictures?

WHY IT MATTERS

Earth is only one of many objects in orbit around the Sun.

SCIENCE WORDS

planet a large body orbiting a star, such as the Sun

solar system a star, such as the Sun, and all the objects orbiting it

asteroid a rocky, metallic object that orbits the Sun

Kepler's laws laws that summarize the movement of the planets

EXPLORE

HYPOTHESIZE How does the sky change from night to night? How do these changes allow you to tell stars from planets? Write a hypothesis in your *Science Journal.* **Test your ideas.**

What Keeps the Planets in Orbit?

The planets and asteroids all travel in orbits around the Sun. An orbit is the path the object travels on. Gravity keeps these objects in their orbits. Without the Sun's gravity, a planet would keep moving in a straight line because of Newton's first law.

The astronomer Johannes Kepler stated three laws that summarize the motion of the planets. The first of **Kepler's laws** as they are called states that planets move on a special path, an ellipse. Law two says that planets move more quickly when they are nearer the Sun. Law three says that the farther away a planet is from the Sun, the longer its year is.

The orbit of a planet is an ellipse.

Why is it important to study the inner planets? Looking at one of Earth's closest neighbors may provide an answer.

Venus has what is known as a runaway greenhouse effect. Infrared light given off by Venus cannot escape its atmosphere. This "trapped" infrared light causes the high temperature on Venus. By studying what happens on Venus, scientists hope to learn how to keep Earth's own greenhouse effect under control.

MATH LINK

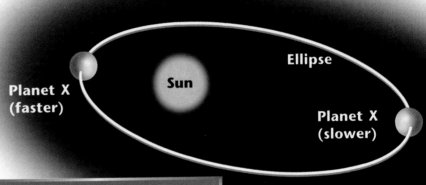

Planet X (faster) · Sun · Ellipse · Planet X (slower)

REVIEW

1. How can we distinguish a planet from a star by looking at its motion?

2. **EXPERIMENT** In the activity on page 335, what is changing from step to step? What effect can this change have?

3. How are the inner planets alike? Different? Include atmospheres in your answer.

4. What is an asteroid?

5. **CRITICAL THINKING** *Apply* What would happen to the planets' orbits if gravity were suddenly shut off?

WHY IT MATTERS THINK ABOUT IT
How might the greenhouse effect cause changes on Earth?

WHY IT MATTERS WRITE ABOUT IT
List the similarities between Earth and Venus. Consider distance from Earth and size. Also consider the presence of atmosphere.

READING SKILL
Compare and contrast any two planets you read about.

Be Your Own Weather Forecaster

"What's the temperature going to be today?" That's the question we most often ask about the weather.

THERMOMETER

Air temperature is measured by a thermometer. The glass tube contains mercury or colored alcohol that expands (rises) or contracts (falls) with temperature changes.

BAROMETER

A barometer measures air pressure—the force on a given area by the weight of air. In one type of barometer, not shown here, mercury in a glass tube is inverted into a reservoir of more mercury. Changes in air pressure cause the mercury to rise and fall.

ANEMOMETER

Winds are described by the direction from which they blow—a north wind comes from the north. Wind vanes show wind direction. An anemometer measures wind speed by counting the revolutions of the cups in a given amount of time.

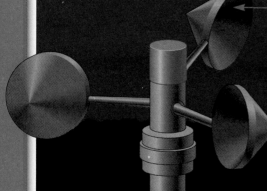

Science, Technology, and Society

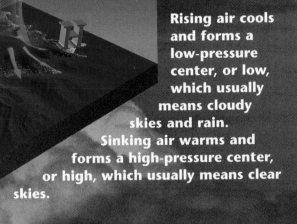

Rising air cools and forms a low-pressure center, or low, which usually means cloudy skies and rain. Sinking air warms and forms a high-pressure center, or high, which usually means clear skies.

HYGROMETER

A hygrometer measures humidity, or the amount of water vapor in the air. It consists of two thermometers, one dry and one covered by a wet sack. The instrument is whirled in the air, and the wet thermometer records a lower temperature. Meteorologists use a chart to convert the difference in temperatures to relative humidity.

DISCUSSION STARTER

1. Collect weather data from any instruments you have at home, and listen to weather reports on TV for five days. Record changes. Are there any patterns to these changes?

2. What are some of the reasons weather prediction is so important?

Different shapes and patterns of clouds can predict a cold front, a warm front, or even a thunderstorm! You can use a cup and ruler to measure precipitation!

To learn more about weather forecasting, visit *www.mhschool.com/science* and select the keyword FORECAST.

*inter***NET**
CONNECTION

WHY IT MATTERS

Some members of the solar system can get very close to Earth.

The Outer Solar System

Have you ever seen a time line? A time line is a way of showing a sequence of events. Here is an example.

Which planet was the first to be discovered in modern times? What does the ragged line just to the left of 1700 mean? Why do you think it took so long to discover the planet Neptune?

SCIENCE WORDS

comet a ball of rock and ice that orbits the Sun

meteoroid a small asteroid (rocky object that orbits the Sun), which may be far out in the solar system or close to the inner planets

meteor a meteoroid that enters Earth's atmosphere and burns with a streak of light

meteorite any part of a meteoroid that reaches Earth's surface

HISTORY LINK

EXPLORE

HYPOTHESIZE How are the planets arranged in the solar system? Does the arrangement help explain why it took so long to discover some of them? Write a hypothesis in your *Science Journal*. Test your ideas.

Mercury

Venus

Mars

DISCOVERY TIME LINE

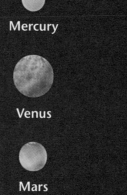

Jupiter

Saturn

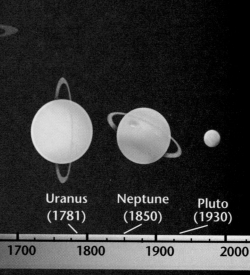

Uranus (1781)

Neptune (1850)

Pluto (1930)

Antiquity   1700   1800   1900   2000

History of Science

Ptolemy

In the second century A.D., Ptolemy described in detail the math behind the theory that the planets moved around Earth.

Hypatia, the first female astronomer, was born in A.D. 370. She invented the plane astrolabe that measured the position of stars, planets, and the Sun. An outraged mob killed her because of her beliefs.

Aryabhata the First (476–550) determined that Earth rotates on its axis. In the 700s Turk Al-Battani calculated the

Copernicus

lengths of a year and of the seasons with great accuracy.

In the 16th century, Copernicus upset the scientific world by suggesting that Aristarchus was correct—that Earth and the other planets orbit the Sun.

A hundred years later, Galileo made one of the first telescopes and used it to prove Copernicus was right. Galileo was imprisoned for his beliefs, making him one of the first heroes of science.

Galileo

Hypatia

DISCUSSION STARTER

1. Compare Aristarchus's theory with Ptolemy's.

2. Why did Copernicus's theory upset the scientific world?

To learn more about astronomy, visit *www.mhschool.com/science* and select the keyword ASTRONOMY.

inter**NET** CONNECTION

WHY IT MATTERS

The Sun is one of billions of stars, the closest to Earth.

SCIENCE WORDS

star a large, hot ball of gases, which is held together by gravity and gives off its own light

parallax the apparent shift in an object's location when viewed from two positions

light-year the distance light travels in a year

constellation a number of stars that appears to form a pattern

magnitude the brightness of a star

nebula a cloud of gas and dust in space

supernova a star that explodes

black hole an object whose gravity is so strong that light cannot escape it

Stars

What are stars? Why do they look like points of light in the night sky?

In the past people saw stars arranged in groups tracing pictures of heroes or other characters. In a star "picture," the stars appear to be side by side against a flat background. That would mean they are all the same distance away from the observer.

Do you think stars really come in groups? Are they all the same distance away?

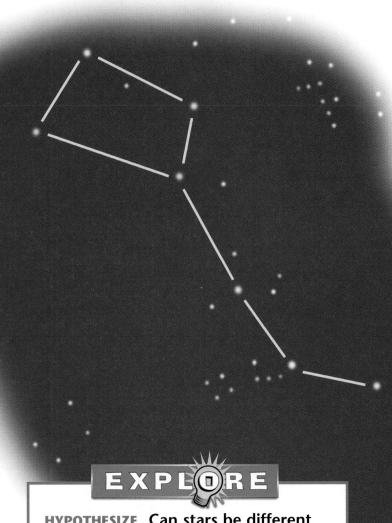

EXPLORE

HYPOTHESIZE Can stars be different distances away and still appear to be side by side? Write a hypothesis in your *Science Journal*. Test your ideas.

Math Link

G stars have calcium, hydrogen, and many metals, particularly iron. These yellow stars are called solar stars because the Sun is one. They have a temperature of about 6,000°C (10,800°F).

F stars are yellow-white stars and have a temperature of about 7,500°C (13,500°F). They have a lot of calcium and hydrogen.

A stars, called white stars, have a lot of hydrogen and a temperature of about 10,000°C (18,000°F). Sirius, an A star, is the brightest star.

DISCUSSION STARTER

1. What did Annie Jump Cannon do to further astronomy?

2. What can scientists tell about stars from analyzing their elements?

B stars have the most helium. These blue-white stars have a temperature of about 20,000°C (36,000°F).

O stars are the hottest, brightest, and largest stars. Called blue giants, these stars are made of helium, oxygen, and nitrogen and have a temperature of about 35,000°C (63,000°F).

To learn more about stars, visit *www.mhschool.com/science* and select the keyword STARCLASS.

*inter***NET** CONNECTION

369

WHY IT MATTERS

With tools and ideas, people are learning more about the universe every day.

SCIENCE WORDS

galaxy a large group of stars held together by gravity

Milky Way our home galaxy

spectrum a band of colors made when white light is broken up

expansion redshift the shift of a spectrum of a galaxy toward longer (redder) wavelengths due to the expansion of space

big bang the beginning of the universe, when the density of the universe was very high

background radiation electromagnetic radiation left over from the big bang

quasar an extremely bright, extremely distant, high-energy source

Galaxies and Beyond

How do you think stars are arranged? Stars are in vast groups in the universe. These groups have immense spaces in between them. The pictures here show the star group that the Sun is in.

Is the Sun at the center of the star group? At the edge? Somewhere in between? If so, how far from the center is the Sun?

EXPLORE

HYPOTHESIZE How can we tell where the Sun is located in this star group? How do we know it is not in any of the other locations? Write a hypothesis in your *Science Journal.* Test your ideas.

SCIENCE WORDS

black hole p.363
comet p.350
galaxy p.372
light-year p.358
meteoroid p.351
nebula p.362

parallax p.358
planet p.334
quasar p.378
solar system p.334
star p.358
supernova p.363

USING SCIENCE WORDS

Number a paper from 1 to 10. Fill in 1 to 5 with words from the list above.

1. The distance to close stars can be measured using ___?___.

2. A distant bright source of high energy is called a(n) ___?___.

3. One type of exploding star is called a(n) ___?___.

4. A group of stars held together by gravity is a(n) ___?___.

5. The Sun and all the objects in orbit around it is the ___?___.

6–10. Pick five words from the list above that were not used in 1 to 5, and use each in a sentence.

UNDERSTANDING SCIENCE IDEAS

11. What object's gravity is so strong that even light cannot escape it?

12. What can we use to predict the motion of planets?

13. What do astronomers call the patterns that we see in the stars?

14. What do astronomers call a meteor that has landed on Earth?

15. What objects in the universe are moving away from each other?

USING IDEAS AND SKILLS

16. The universe is expanding. What evidence supports this theory?

17. **READING SKILL: COMPARE AND CONTRAST** How is the speed of a planet related to its distance from the Sun?

18. What are the possible final states of a star?

19. **EXPERIMENT** What determines whether an object falls to Earth's surface or orbits Earth?

20. **THINKING LIKE A SCIENTIST** The galaxies are moving away from each other. What force acts to oppose this expansion? Is this the same force that causes a ball to return to Earth after it is thrown upward?

PROBLEMS and PUZZLES

Sky View Borrow some binoculars, go as far from city lights as you can, and observe the night sky. What stars can you identify? Use a star map as a guide, if you can.

SCIENCE WORDS

asteroid p.340

comet p.350

galaxy p.372

meteorite p.351

refraction p.294

revolution p.312

rotation p.308

solar eclipse p.323

supernova p.363

tide p.324

USING SCIENCE WORDS

Number a paper from 1 to 10. Beside each number write the word or words that best complete the sentence.

1. The bending of waves as they go from one substance to another is called __?__.

2. A complete spin of a planet on its axis is called a(n) __?__.

3. A complete trip around the Sun is called __?__.

4. A blocking out of a view of the Sun when Earth passes through the Moon's shadow is a(n) __?__.

5. The Moon's gravity (pull) causes ocean __?__.

6. A rocky, metallic object that orbits the Sun is a(n) __?__.

7. After a meteor hits Earth, whatever is left is called a(n) __?__.

8. The tail or tails of a __?__ always point away from the Sun.

9. A star that explodes is a(n) __?__.

10. The Milky Way is our __?__.

UNDERSTANDING SCIENCE IDEAS

Write 11 to 15. For each number write the letter for the best answer. You may wish to use the hints provided.

11. Kepler's model of the solar system is not correct because
    a. it is too small
    b. it is too old
    c. it uses geometric shapes
    d. it contradicts observations
    (Hint: Read page 293.)

12. Planets were noticeably different from stars to ancient peoples because
    a. planets "wandered" among stars
    b. planets appeared to be smaller than stars
    c. stars were farther away
    d. the skies were much clearer
    (Hint: Read page 334.)

13. Galileo discovered that Jupiter
    a. had moons
    b. was made of asteroids
    c. was covered with ice
    d. had rings
    (Hint: Read page 352.)

14. The brightness of a star is its
    a. parallax
    b. magnitude
    c. phase
    d. wavelength
    (Hint: Read page 359.)

15. The universe is
    a. a galaxy
    b. getting larger all the time
    c. the result of a red shift
    d. getting denser as it gets older
    (Hint: Read page 375.)

USING IDEAS AND SKILLS

16.  **MAKE A MODEL** What is a common model of Earth? What is the difference between a model and the real thing?

17. Why are standard time zones 15° wide in longitude?

18. How is a sundial used to tell time?

19. How does a solar eclipse happen?

20. How are comets and asteroids alike? How are they different?

21. List the planets Saturn, Jupiter, and Uranus in order of their distance from the Sun. Label one biggest, another smallest.

22. How is Pluto different from the other outer planets?

23. What theory did the discovery of the background radiation help support? Explain.

THINKING LIKE A SCIENTIST

24.  **EXPERIMENT** The stars in a constellation seem to be close together. How could you demonstrate that they are not close but can appear to be.

25. What happens to a spectrum of light from a galaxy that is moving away from our viewpoint?

WRITING IN YOUR JOURNAL

SCIENCE IN YOUR LIFE
Describe one way that space exploration has changed the way people communicate with each other around the world.

SCIENCE TODAY/TOMORROW
Why do you think people are interested in learning more about other planets? Why might you want to explore a planet one day? What might you wonder that you'd find?

HOW SCIENTISTS WORK
Why do you think people were able to describe stars and planets long before telescopes were invented?

Design your own Experiment

A sundial allows you to tell time when the Sun is up. Can you think of a way to tell time from the sky at night? Check with your teacher before carrying out the experiment.

inter**NET** CONNECTION

For help in reviewing this unit, visit *www.mhschool.com/science*

PROBLEMS and PUZZLES

Life on Earth-2

The planet Earth-2 is just like Earth in almost every way. It has the same size, shape, atmosphere, and distance to its sun as Earth. There is one characteristic that Earth-2 does not share with Earth: Earth-2 has no seasons. There is no winter or summer on Earth-2. The temperatures at any place tend to be the same all year round. Can you think of a reason why Earth-2 might not have seasons? Include a diagram in your explanation.

Earth-2, similar to Earth in almost every way

Star Puzzle

Three stars—star A, star B, and star C—are all visible in the night sky. In apparent magnitude—how bright the stars appear to be—A seems brighter than B and less bright than C. In absolute magnitude—how much light energy the stars actually give off—A is brighter than C but less bright than B.

Which star is closest to Earth? Farthest from Earth? Use the information above and the table to determine the relative distance of each star from Earth. Rank each star from 1 to 3 in each category.

Star	Apparent Magnitude (how bright it appears)	Absolute Magnitude (how bright it really is)	Closeness
A			
B			
C			

Marble Drop

SAFETY Wear goggles.

Pour about 3 cm of aquarium gravel into a deep 6- to 9-in. pie tin. On top of the gravel place about 3 cm of flour. Over the flour sprinkle a very thin layer of fine soil or powdered cocoa. Place the pie tin in the center of a large sheet of newspaper. Drop a marble from a height of 50 cm into the center of your pie tin. Carefully remove the marble. Do this several times. You can also vary the height or angle at which your marble hits the pie tin. Describe how this model suggests how craters on the Moon, Mercury, and the moons of the outer planets may have formed.

Physical Science Link

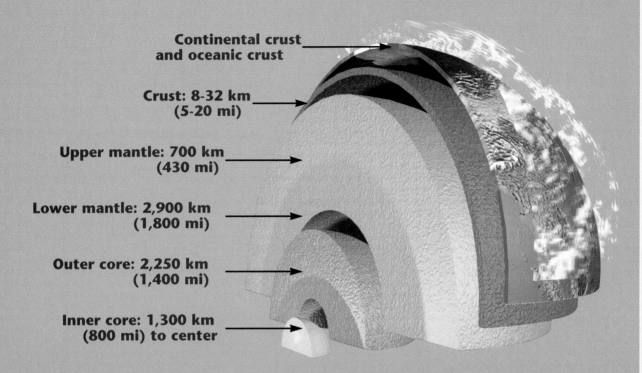

Continental crust and oceanic crust

Crust: 8-32 km
(5-20 mi)

Upper mantle: 700 km
(430 mi)

Lower mantle: 2,900 km
(1,800 mi)

Outer core: 2,250 km
(1,400 mi)

Inner core: 1,300 km
(800 mi) to center

By comparing P and S waves traveling through Earth, scientists have made models of Earth's insides. In 1906 P waves located the boundary between Earth's core and mantle. Three years later P and S waves determined the boundary between Earth's crust and mantle.

Scientists also tracked seismic waves to learn about Earth's outer and inner cores.

In 1926 a scientist discovered that S waves didn't go through Earth's core. Conclusion? The outer core is liquid. In 1936 another scientist tracked P waves that reached Earth's core. Conclusion? The inner core must be solid!

DISCUSSION STARTER

1. How can P and S waves determine boundaries of inner Earth?

2. Do you think scientists will ever have actual evidence of what's in Earth's core? Why or why not?

S waves can't move through liquid.

P waves can move through liquid.

Bending of waves

To learn more about what's inside Earth, visit *www.mhschool.com/science* and select the keyword CORE.

WHY IT MATTERS

While volcanoes can be dangerous, they provide energy and resources.

SCIENCE WORDS

hot spot a very hot part of the mantle, where magma can melt through a plate moving above it

vent a central opening in a volcanic area through which magma may escape

lava magma that reaches Earth's surface and flows out of a vent

crater a cuplike hollow that forms at the top of a volcano around the vent

cinder-cone volcano a steep-sided cone that forms from explosive eruptions of hot rocks, ranging from particles to boulders

shield volcano a wide, gently sloped cone that forms from flows of lava

composite volcano a cone formed from explosive eruptions of hot rocks followed by a flow of lava, over and over

geothermal energy heat from below Earth's surface

Volcanoes

Where are volcanoes located? Can any volcano erupt at any time? Are some more likely to erupt than others?

Mount Etna, in Italy, has the longest record of eruptions in history. Since the first recorded eruption in 1500 B.C., Mount Etna has erupted 190 times! The most recent string of eruptions stretches back over decades. Recent eruptions have included fire fountains in early 1996. However, Mount Etna is not alone. All told, Italy has 13 active volcanoes!

EXPLORE

HYPOTHESIZE Where are volcanoes found on Earth's crust? Are volcanoes more common in certain places than others? Write a hypothesis in your *Science Journal*. How can you test your ideas?

volcanoes may have beautifully symmetrical shapes. That is, the shape on one side of the cone matches the shape on the opposite side.

Sometimes an eruption "takes turns." An eruption may explode. It sends gas and lava high into the air and forms a rain of rocks of different sizes. Then the eruption may switch over to a quiet period. Lava may flow over the rocks from the explosive period. When this switching repeats over and over, it forms a composite volcano.

Brain Power

What properties, if any, do the three kinds of cones have in common? What properties do they not have in common?

Layers of rock fragments and lava

Magma

Shishaldin is a composite volcano.

QUICK LAB

Cones

MATH LINK

HYPOTHESIZE How are volcanic cones different? Write a hypothesis in your *Science Journal.*

MATERIALS
- modeling compound
- sand, soil, or gravel
- water
- paper towels
- *Science Journal*

PROCEDURES

1. **MAKE A MODEL** Build models of the three kinds of cones. Choose materials that show the differences. (Use water to hold particles together.)

2. Draw diagrams of your finished products in your *Science Journal.*

CONCLUDE AND APPLY

1. **EVALUATE** How well do the models show the differences?

2. How else could you show the differences between cones?

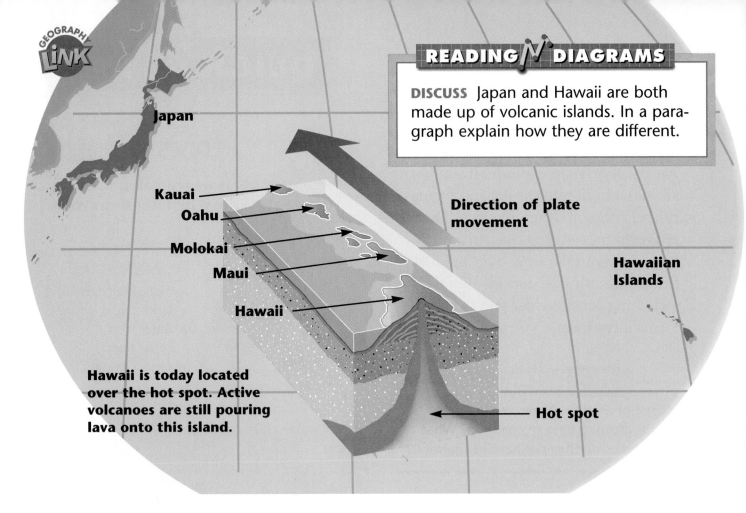

Japan

READING DIAGRAMS

DISCUSS Japan and Hawaii are both made up of volcanic islands. In a paragraph explain how they are different.

Kauai

Oahu

Molokai

Maui

Hawaii

Direction of plate movement

Hawaiian Islands

Hawaii is today located over the hot spot. Active volcanoes are still pouring lava onto this island.

Hot spot

Are All Volcanoes Active?

Thousands of volcanoes are scattered over Earth's surface. However, very few of them are active. That is, very few are erupting now or have erupted recently. Many of Earth's active volcanoes are located in the Pacific Ring of Fire. For example, there are active volcanoes in Japan.

Japan is made up of volcanic islands. These islands were built up from the ocean floor along a convergent boundary. One plate is plunging down under another. Molten rock pushed through to the surface and formed a string, or arc, of volcanoes. The volcanoes grew in size over time, from undersea volcanoes to islands far above sea level.

In time active volcanoes may stop erupting. They may become *dormant*. *Dormant* is from a French word for "sleep." A dormant volcano has not been active for a long period of time but has erupted in recorded history.

Some volcanoes are considered *extinct*. An extinct volcano has not erupted in recorded history.

The Hawaiian Islands are volcanic islands. Many of these volcanoes are no longer active. The Hawaiian Islands, remember, were formed as the Pacific plate moved over a hot spot. The island of Kauai (kou´ī) is the oldest island. It formed when it was located over the hot spot. As the plate moved, Kauai moved away from the hot spot and was no longer active. The plate continued to move, and other islands formed, one at a time.

What Happens Underground?

Sometimes underground magma cools and hardens before it reaches the surface. Magma can harden in many possible shapes and positions.

A *dike* is formed when magma hardens in vertical cracks. Dikes are vertical or nearly vertical structures. A *sill* is formed when magma hardens between horizontal layers of rock. A sill is flat. Dikes and sills vary in size from small to huge. When rocks around a large dike are worn away, the dike is exposed as a long ridge. Exposed sills take the shape of ridges or cliffs.

If the magma pushed into a sill is thick, it may not spread far horizontally. Instead it pushes upward, forming a *laccolith.* A laccolith is shaped like a dome.

When magma pushes upward, it raises overlying rock layers into *dome mountains.* A dome mountain is a broad, circular mountain formed from uplifted rock layers. The Henry Mountains of Utah were formed by laccoliths. Some dome mountains, like the Black Hills of South Dakota, were formed from layers that became folded.

The largest and deepest of all underground formations are *batholiths.* A batholith is huge and irregularly shaped. It reaches deep into the crust. Some batholiths have been uplifted to above sea level. As overlying rocks were worn away, the batholiths became exposed. They look like large, steep hills.

Batholiths have been found in many great mountain ranges. Sierra Nevada in California contains a number of batholiths covering an area of over 40,000 square kilometers (15,444 square miles).

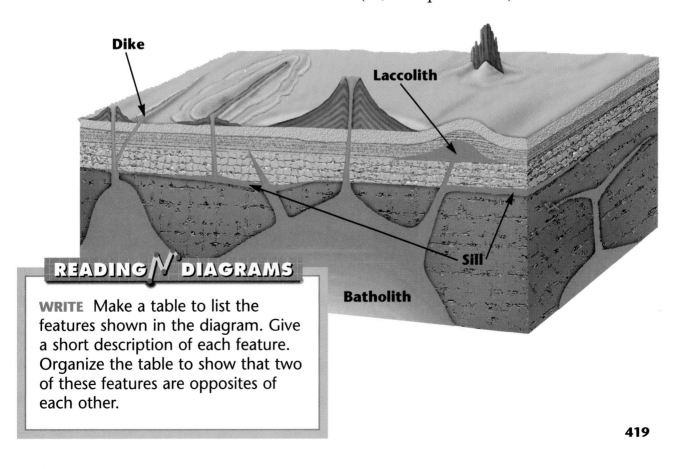

Dike

Laccolith

Sill

Batholith

READING /N DIAGRAMS

WRITE Make a table to list the features shown in the diagram. Give a short description of each feature. Organize the table to show that two of these features are opposites of each other.

Can Magma Heat Water?

Perhaps the most spectacular side effect of volcanism is a *geyser*. A geyser is an opening in the ground through which hot water and steam erupt periodically. The main vent of a geyser is filled with water. The water at the bottom of the column is heated and changed to steam. At first the steam is held down by the weight of the water above it. Pressure continues to build up as more water is changed to steam. It is like shaking a bottle of soda with the cap still on.

Finally, some steam pushes high enough to move the column of water. This action relieves some pressure. A jet of hot water and steam soon erupts from the geyser. After the geyser erupts, the vent fills with more water, and the cycle begins again.

Hot springs are also caused by underground heating. A hot spring is an opening in the ground where hot water and gases escape. The water is heated deep underground by magma. The heated water is forced up to an opening in the surface. The water may contain minerals. As the water cools, it may deposit a spectacular mineral load.

Sometimes the water evaporates quickly as it flows out. The remaining water may become thick with broken pieces of rock and minerals. The result is a hot, muddy pool, called a paint pot. The materials mixed in the water may make it look yellow, red, or black.

Can the heat from such hot springs and geysers be used? Today scientists are finding ways to use **geothermal energy**. Geothermal energy is heat from below Earth's surface.

READING 📈 DIAGRAMS

WRITE In a paragraph explain what is happening in the diagram. Include a description of what happens before the event shown.

A geyser

In 1965 the first geothermal power plant in the United States was built in Healdsburg, California. Wells were dug to hot rock material below the surface. Steam was produced. It was used to run power plants that produced electricity.

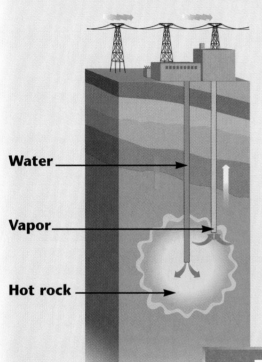

Water is changed to steam by being heated below the surface. The steam can run a power plant.

Water

Vapor

Hot rock

WHY IT MATTERS

Did you know that the United States ranks third (after Indonesia and Japan) in the number of historically active volcanoes? Volcanic eruptions have created many valuable natural resources. For example, volcanic ash falling on the land around a volcano increases soil fertility. Forests and farm crops grow better because the ash adds nutrients and acts as a mulch.

Underground magma heats groundwater. The heated water can be used as a source of heat, or geothermal energy. Heated groundwater also concentrates valuable minerals such as copper, tin, gold, and silver. Over many thousands of years, these minerals built up into deposits that are mined.

READING DIAGRAMS

WRITE In a paragraph explain what is shown by the arrows in the diagram.

REVIEW

1. Are volcanoes distributed randomly or in a pattern?

2. List the parts of a volcano.

3. Why are there different kinds of volcanoes?

4. **COMPARE AND CONTRAST** Describe the different kinds of underground features caused by volcanoes.

5. **CRITICAL THINKING** *Synthesize* How do volcanoes support the theory of plate tectonics?

WHY IT MATTERS THINK ABOUT IT
Do you live near a volcano? If so, what is it like? If not, how far are you from one? What would it be like to visit one?

WHY IT MATTERS WRITE ABOUT IT
How are volcanoes dangerous? How can they be helpful? Write a composition comparing the effects.

Disaster Alerts

Scientists can predict weather disasters, like tornadoes and hurricanes, thanks to modern technology. Can they also tell when there'll be a volcanic eruption or earthquake, and alert people to the danger?

Predicting Eruptions

In the past when a volcano erupted, there was no escape. Today almost all eruptions can be predicted early enough to warn people.

How do scientists know there might be an eruption? Magma moving inside a volcano causes patterns of small earthquakes that create a steady roar. Nearby seismographs record that magma is on the move. Scientists warn people to leave the area. That's how

30,000 people were saved in 1994 when a giant volcano erupted in New Guinea.

Sometimes a volcano explodes through the side of its cone. Before it blows, a buildup of gases bulges the side. Lasers record ground swells around volcanoes to the nearest millimeter. Satellite radar detects even the tiniest ground motion. These clues predict which side of the cone will blow.

The Dante 2 robot goes into a volcano's crater to measure gases. The composition of gases may predict an eruption.

In 1980 scientists predicted that Mount Saint Helens would erupt, but not exactly when.

Science, Technology, and Society

Predicting Earthquakes

Earthquake prediction is still difficult, but one prediction was a big success. In 1975 the Chinese noted changing water levels in their wells, odd behavior of domestic animals, and a series of small earthquakes. All this evidence predicted a great earthquake would hit Lianong Province. People were warned to get outside of buildings. When the earthquake came, only 300 people were killed. The following year 750,000 Chinese were killed in an unpredicted earthquake in Tangshan.

The map on page 402, Topic 2, showed where earthquake zones are located. There, minor earthquakes are common. California's an exception. It's been hit with destructive earthquakes every 15 years or so for the last century!

DISCUSSION STARTER

1. A volcano covers a small area, while an earthquake zone may be hundreds of kilometers long. How does this affect the amount of destruction each can cause?

2. Do you think it's easier to predict floods, hurricanes, and tornadoes than volcanic eruptions or earthquakes? Why?

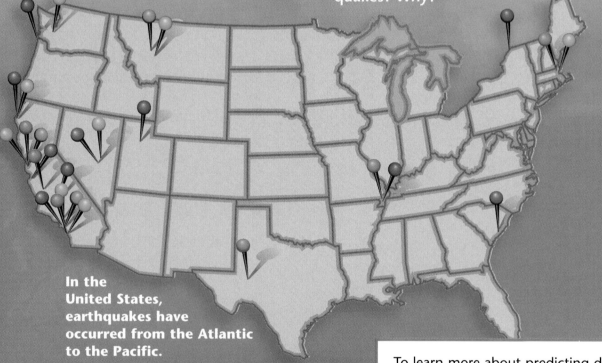

In the United States, earthquakes have occurred from the Atlantic to the Pacific.

To learn more about predicting disasters, visit *www.mhschool.com/science* and select the keyword DISASTER.

*inter*NET
CONNECTION

SCIENCE WORDS

crust p.388

epicenter p.404

fault p.403

hot spot p.414

lava p.415

magma p.390

magnitude p.407

mantle p.393

plate
  tectonics p.393

seismograph p.405

subduction p.396

USING SCIENCE WORDS

Number a paper from 1 to 10. Fill in 1 to 5 with words from the list above.

1. The modern idea of crustal motion is ___?___.

2. Magma that reaches the surface becomes ___?___.

3. The plunging of one plate under another is ___?___.

4. The Hawaiian Islands formed over a(n) ___?___.

5. The point where an earthquake begins is the ___?___.

6–10. Pick five words from the list above that were not used in 1 to 5, and use each in a sentence.

UNDERSTANDING SCIENCE IDEAS

11. Which waves from an earthquake arrive first?

12. What is the surface of Earth called?

13. How do earthquakes affect the oceans?

14. Name three kinds of volcanic cones.

15. What are the two uppermost layers of Earth?

USING IDEAS AND SKILLS

16. **READING SKILL: CAUSE AND EFFECT** How is new rock being formed at the sea floor?

17. How do waves from an earthquake give information about the earthquake? Tell what kind of information it gives.

18. Why do volcanoes erupt? How do they erupt in different ways?

19. **HYPOTHESIZE** Copy the table. Describe a hypothesis that ties together all the ideas in the table. In each column tell how the hypothesis explains the idea at the top. Add columns to the table as needed. Give the table a name.

	Earthquakes	Volcanoes
Continent		
Coastlines		

20. **THINKING LIKE A SCIENTIST** How do scientists make predictions about plate tectonics in the future? What kind of data do they need to collect to make predictions?

PROBLEMS and PUZZLES

Rock Rumble Volcanism on Earth is an ongoing process. In contrast most of the volcanism on the Moon occurred between three and four billion years ago. How would scientists know this? What differences do you think there are between volcanic activity on Earth and on the Moon?

R.I.P

CHAPTER 10
HOW EARTH CHANGES OVER TIME

The walls of the Grand Canyon give many clues to the passage of time in North America. Each layer is like a huge chapter of history.

How do you think the layers got here? How did the layers become exposed? As a clue look at the bottom of the canyon.

In this chapter you will read about events happening in order, that is, sequence of events.

WHY IT MATTERS

Soil is needed for things to grow.

SCIENCE WORDS

fold mountain a mountain made mostly of rock layers folded by being squeezed together

fault-block mountain a mountain made by huge tilted blocks of rocks separated from surrounding rocks by faults

weathering the breaking down of rocks into smaller pieces by natural processes

erosion the picking up and removal of rock particles

soil a mixture of weathered rock, decayed plant and animal matter, living things, air, and water

soil horizon any of the layers of soil from the surface to the bedrock below

groundwater water that soaks into soil and rock by collecting in spaces between rock particles

humus material in soil formed by the breakdown of plant and animal material

Building Up and Breaking Down

Have you ever seen mountains in the distance? Up close? From above in a jet? In movies? What shapes do they have? Are the shapes alike or different? Why do you think mountains have the shapes they have?

For example, here are two mountains that look very different from each other. What kinds of processes form mountains such as these? Are there different processes at work forming different kinds of mountains?

EXPLORE

HYPOTHESIZE What kinds of processes could make mountains? Can different processes produce different kinds of mountains? Write a hypothesis in your *Science Journal.* Test your ideas.

Investigate How a Mountain Is Made

Use a model to infer how mountains can be made.

MATERIALS

- waxed paper
- clay
- 2 sturdy wooden rulers
- scissors
- plastic knife (optional)
- *Science Journal*

PROCEDURES

SAFETY Be careful with sharp objects.

1. MAKE A MODEL Use the clay to make four thin (0.5-cm thick) square layers. They should be the same size (about 6–8 cm on a side).

2. COMMUNICATE Stack the four layers. Pinch them together along opposite sides. Place them on a sheet of waxed paper cut to fit the bottom of the layers. In your *Science Journal,* draw a picture of the clay layers.

3. Place the waxed paper and clay on the table. You need to see the layers. Place the pinched-together sides of the clay against the two rulers.

4. COMPARE Slowly move one ruler toward the other. Observe what happens. Draw a picture of the results.

CONCLUDE AND APPLY

1. OBSERVE What happened to the clay as you moved the ruler?

2. DRAW CONCLUSIONS What does this result tell you about what happens when bendable objects are squeezed from both sides?

3. INFER Can rocks bend? How do you know?

GOING FURTHER: Problem Solving

4. USE VARIABLES What if a fault (crack) had been cut through the layers before they were squeezed? How might your results differ?

How Is a Mountain Made?

As the crust moves, the rocks of the crust can change. They can change position. They can move up, down, or sideways. Rocks can also change their shape. They can be bent, squeezed, twisted, or broken. These changes can cause different types of features to be made. The Explore Activity showed one example of how this happens.

The most common type of mountain is a **fold mountain**. A fold mountain is a mountain made mostly of rock layers folded by being squeezed together.

A **fault-block mountain** is a mountain made by huge tilted blocks of rocks separated from surrounding rock by faults. A fault is a large crack in rocks along which there is movement.

FAULT-BLOCK MOUNTAINS

The Grand Tetons of Wyoming are fault-block mountains.

Cross section of a fault-block mountain

FOLD MOUNTAINS

The Appalachian Mountains are fold mountains.

Cross section of a fold mountain

How Do Streams Change?

A river or stream carries sediment downhill and deposits it elsewhere. As a result the river or stream changes. Deep, fast streams become slower and shallower.

Curves develop. Water flows faster along the outside of a curve and eats away at it. On the inside of a curve, the water slows down and drops off sediment.

A river may have all these stages along its path. Some rivers are entirely one or two stages.

Flatter, slower-moving stage

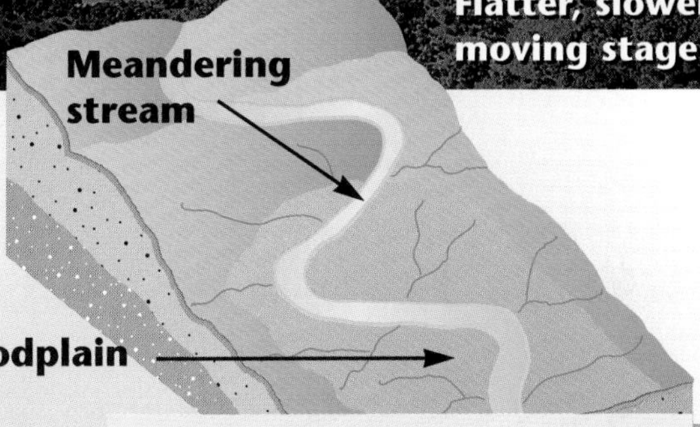

Meandering stream

Floodplain

- **The path is flatter because the river has worn down the land.**
- **Curves (called *meanders*) develop.**
- **The river is slower and deposits much sediment.**
- **The river is shallower and wider.**
- **Flat plains develop on the sides of the river.**

Steep, fast-moving stage

No floodplain

Rapids

READING / DIAGRAMS

1. **DISCUSS** What are the main ways a river changes from stage to stage?
2. **REPRESENT** Draw a diagram of a way to see all these changes using a large tray of moistened soil.

- **The river flows along a steep path.**
- **The path is straight.**
- **The water is fast moving and carries much sediment.**
- **The river cuts down into the bottom. It forms steep valleys with a V shape.**

How Does Moving Ice Shape the Land?

The huge sheets of ice you see here are like giant bulldozers. They are moving and can move rocks and sediment. These huge moving sheets of ice are **glaciers**. To know how glaciers can move, you have to understand how they form.

Some glaciers form in valleys high up in the mountains. Others form near the poles. Glaciers form when more snow falls in the winter than melts in the summer. Over time the snow gets deeper and deeper.

Newly fallen snow is fluffy because it has air trapped inside. As snow piles up though, the weight of the snow on top squeezes the snow at the bottom into a solid mass of ice. When the ice gets to be about 100 meters (328 feet) thick, it can move. The weight above makes the ice at the bottom like a superthick syrup. The whole sheet of ice then moves downhill.

SOME FACTS ABOUT GLACIERS

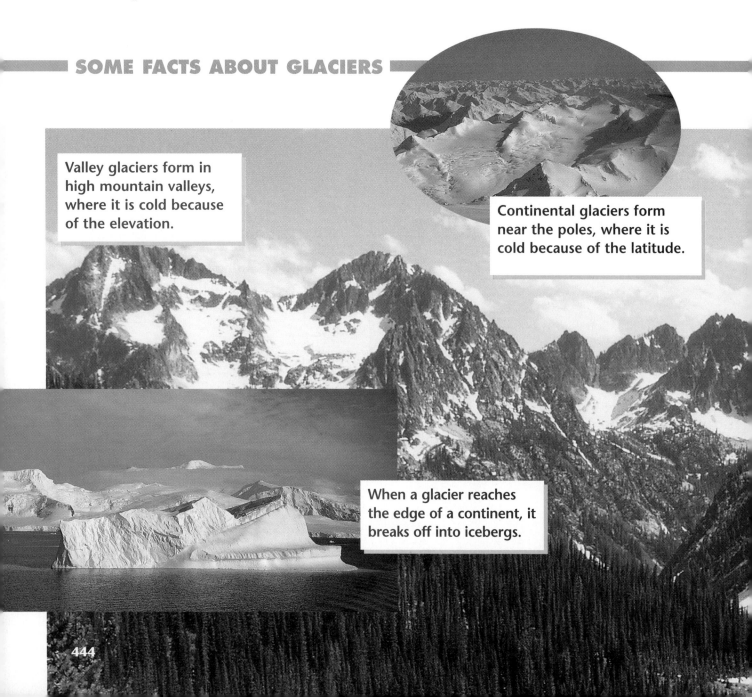

Valley glaciers form in high mountain valleys, where it is cold because of the elevation.

Continental glaciers form near the poles, where it is cold because of the latitude.

When a glacier reaches the edge of a continent, it breaks off into icebergs.

Glaciers Carry Rocks

Glaciers move like huge, slow bulldozers. They can push loose rocks and soil out of their path. They drag sediment underneath. Loose rocks and soil get pushed up in piles along the front and sides of the glacier.

When a glacier moves over the ground, pieces of rock may freeze into the ice. If a rock freezes into the glacier, it can be "plucked" out of the ground as the glacier moves along. In this way huge chunks of rock may be picked up and carried great distances.

The rocks along the bottom and sides of a glacier can scrape against the land. They are like the blades of a huge plow. Any layers that a glacier passes over may be deeply scratched. Some exposed rock in a valley floor may become polished smooth.

As a glacier moves through a valley, it digs deep into the walls and floor. A once-narrow valley that had a V shape becomes wider. As a glacier moves through, the valley becomes U shaped.

Narrower glaciers dragged soil along. As they merged into one glacier, the soil became trapped in the middle, like a stream of soil.

What clues can tell that a glacier once moved through this valley?

445

What Happens when Glaciers Melt?

Glaciers eventually reach places where it is warm, and they melt. When the ice melts, the rocks that were frozen into it fall to the ground in a jumble. It is a jumble of many sizes of sediment, known as till.

A deposit of many sizes of sediment from a glacier that collects in front of or along the sides of the glacier is called moraine (mə rān'). As the glacier melts away, the moraine is left behind as mounds or long ridges.

As a glacier melts, meltwater flows out from the edges of the glacier. This water carries sediment from the glacier. The water may carry the sedi-ment for some distance before dropping it off. The result may be a wide, flat plain in front of a glacier covered with layers of sediment.

Sometimes chunks of ice get buried in till. When ice chunks finally melt, the till above them collapses, forming a bowl-like hole in the ground. These holes may fill up with water, forming ponds or lakes.

Glaciers also form lakes in other ways. Sometimes they scrape huge holes in the ground. The holes fill up with meltwater when the glacier melts. Also moraines act as dams. They trap flowing meltwater into lakes.

Some piles of till get smoothed out if a glacier flows over them. These teardrop-shaped piles of till are called drumlins.

HOW GLACIERS CHANGE THE LAND

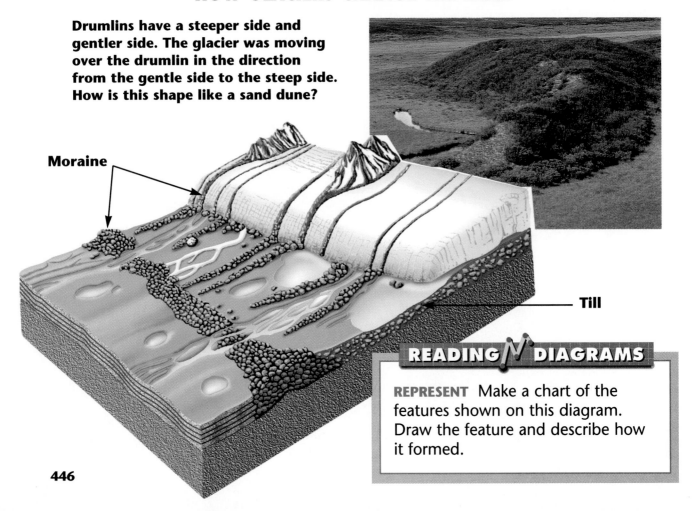

Drumlins have a steeper side and gentler side. The glacier was moving over the drumlin in the direction from the gentle side to the steep side. How is this shape like a sand dune?

Moraine

Till

READING DIAGRAMS

REPRESENT Make a chart of the features shown on this diagram. Draw the feature and describe how it formed.

What Have Glaciers Left Behind?

For long times during Earth's history, glaciers covered much of the land. These periods of time are called ice ages. Glaciers from the last ice age began to melt back, or retreat, about 20,000 years ago.

These glaciers left behind a lot of sand, gravel, and clay. These are valuable natural resources. Clay deposited in glacial lakes can be used to make bricks, pottery, and concrete. Sand and gravel is used to make concrete for buildings and roads.

Glacial lake

Erosion and deposition are a part of your world. If you live near a river, that river is a product of these forces. Glaciers may have carried valuable soil to your area in the past.

Do you live in Detroit, Chicago, Cleveland, Buffalo, or any of the other cities along these lakes? If so, thank a glacier for making your home possible. Why? The Great Lakes are five glacial lakes. They are the world's largest single source of fresh water. Also they provide easy transport routes. That is why these lakes are ideal locations for cities.

☐ Ocean

☐ Continental glacier

▨ Nonglaciated land

Glaciers covered much of North America 20,000 years ago.

REVIEW

1. How can wind and gravity change Earth's surface?

2. How can flowing water cause erosion?

3. What can happen as a glacier moves through an area?

4. **CAUSE AND EFFECT** Why do glaciers form only in certain areas?

5. **CRITICAL THINKING** *Analyze* How can a slow-moving river be made fast moving? Explain your answer.

WHY IT MATTERS **THINK ABOUT IT**
What if there was a heavy rainstorm or strong wind in your area? How could it cause erosion and deposition?

WHY IT MATTERS **WRITE ABOUT IT**
How are rivers important in the economics of a country? How can strong winds affect the economics of a country?

Mapping Earth's Topography

What's topography? It's what's on Earth's surface! A topographical map shows the features of an area, such as mountains, bridges, buildings, and lakes. It also shows any changes in elevation—height above or below sea level. Contour lines connect places that have the same elevation. You can make a topographical map.

WHAT YOU NEED

▶ clear-plastic box with lid

▶ modeling clay

▶ marker

▶ ruler

▶ water

▶ pencil

WHAT YOU DO:

1. Mark elevations of 0, 1, ..., 10 cm on the outside of the box.

2. Build a clay island inside the box.

3. Pour water up to the 1-cm mark.

4. Use a pencil to scratch a shoreline contour line around the island.

5. Fill the box with water, 1 cm at a time. Scratch contour lines, too.

6. Pour out the water, then place the lid on the box.

7. Trace a map of the island's contour lines on the lid of the box.

Geography Link

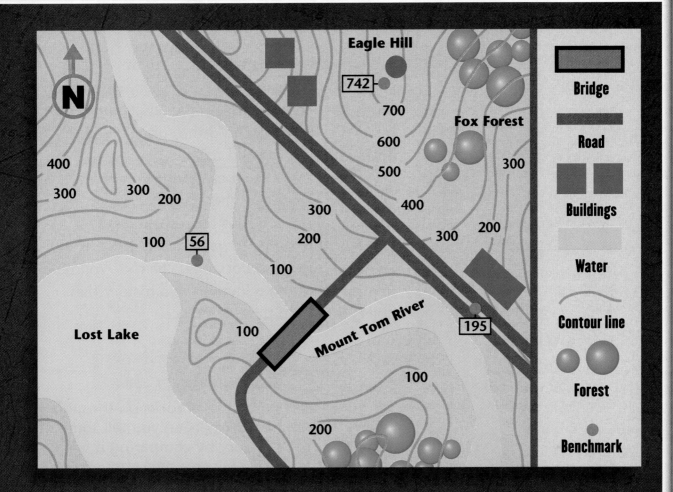

Look at this topographical map. It shows benchmarks—places with carefully measured elevations—as well as contour lines. Use the map to help you answer these questions.

1. How many benchmarks are on the map?

2. What's the highest elevation?

3. What's the contour interval, or difference in elevation between neighboring contour lines?

4. How many buildings are above the 500-meter contour line?

5. What's the elevation of Lost Lake?

6. Imagine you're sailing south on Mount Tom River. Describe the changes in scene as you go.

DISCUSSION STARTER

Would a topographical map be useful if you planned to spend a day at the beach? On a hike? Why or why not?

To learn more about topography, visit *www.mhschool.com/science* and select the keyword TOPOGRAPHY.

*inter*NET
CONNECTION

WHY IT MATTERS

Rocks come in many types and have many uses.

SCIENCE WORDS

mineral a naturally occurring solid in Earth's crust with a definite structure and composition

igneous rock a rock that forms when hot, liquid rock material cools and hardens into a solid

sedimentary rock a rock that forms from pieces of other rocks that are squeezed or cemented together

metamorphic rock a rock that forms from another kind of rock that is changed by heat or pressure or by a chemical reaction

rock cycle rocks continually changing from one kind into another in a never-ending process

The Rock Cycle

What is happening here? You're watching solid rock forming before your very eyes. The red-hot material is molten rock that comes from below Earth's surface. At the surface it cools and hardens into solid rock.

Where do you see rocks around you? Have you ever wondered where a rock came from? What kind of processes form rocks? A rock is like a history book. It was formed and it was changed by many processes. The rock you hold in your hand today may have a history that goes far back in time and place.

EXPLORE

HYPOTHESIZE Do all rocks go through the same history? Can you tell some of a rock's history by comparing it with other rocks? Write a hypothesis in your *Science Journal*. Test your ideas.

Basalt (bə sôlt')

Andesite (an'də lzīt')

Coquina (kō kē'nə)

EXPLORE ACTIVITY

Investigate What the Properties of Rocks Are

Look for similarities and differences between rocks to infer how the rocks may have formed and changed.

MATERIALS

- rock samples
- goggles
- clear tape
- marker
- hand lens
- plastic knife
- index cards
- 2 Tbsp. of sand in plastic cup (optional)
- *Science Journal*

PROCEDURES

 SAFETY Wear goggles.

1. **OBSERVE** Tag each sample with an ID number. Look carefully at each sample. Use a hand lens to observe details.

2. **OBSERVE** How rough is the surface of each sample? Try scratching each rock gently with a plastic knife.

3. **MAKE DECISIONS** What characteristics can you use to tell your rocks apart? Color? Size of pieces that make up the rock? Roughness? Any other? Make a list in your *Science Journal*.

4. **COMMUNICATE** Construct your own data table to record the characteristics of your samples.

Sandstone

CONCLUDE AND APPLY

1. **EVALUATE** Write a description of each sample on a card. Do not include the ID number. Ask a partner to match the cards and samples. The better your partner does, the better your descriptions are. How well did you do?

2. **COMPARE AND CONTRAST** Which rocks shown here are similar to any of your samples? Explain your answer.

3. **DRAW CONCLUSIONS** Do you think all your rocks have a similar history? Explain your answer based on your results.

Granite

GOING FURTHER: Problem Solving

4. **HYPOTHESIZE** How could you turn a cup of sand into a rock? Share your ideas with others and your teacher before trying it.

Conglomerate

Marble

What Are the Properties of Rocks?

How would you know a rock when you saw one? You would need to know the properties of rocks. The Explore Activity deals with some of these properties. To begin with, rocks are solids. They make up Earth's crust. Look closely at many rocks and you see **minerals** in them. A mineral is a naturally occurring solid with a definite structure. Each mineral is made up of particular elements. It is not made of any matter that was once living, like decayed bone or shells.

A rock can be one mineral or a mixture of minerals. You can tell minerals apart by their structure and properties. You can see a crystal structure in the minerals shown here—a geometric shape coming from the way atoms are arranged inside.

Properties include *hardness*, a measure of how easily a mineral can be scratched. Another property is *luster*, how a mineral reflects light. A mineral may shine like a metal or be dull, silky, or glassy. The *streak* of a mineral is its color when it is ground into a powder.

Feldspar

Mica

Hornblende

Quartz

This rock, granite, is a mixture of minerals.

Talc, the softest mineral, has a silky luster.

THE HARDNESS SCALE

Each object on the list can scratch items below it. The tools (nail, penny, file, and so on) are used to help tell the hardness of the minerals.

Mineral	Tool	Hardness
Talc		1.0
Gypsum		2.0
	fingernail	2.5
Calcite		3.0
	copper penny	3.5
Fluorite		4.0
	iron nail	4.5
Apatite		5.0
Glass		5.5
Feldspar		6.0
	steel file	6.5
Quartz		7.0
	porcelain streak plate	7.0
Topaz		8.0
Corundum		9.0
Diamond		10.0

Diamond, the hardest mineral, has a glassy or brilliant luster.

Math Link

This player's batting average is expressed as a ratio.

If a recipe reads, "Use 1 part cranberry juice to 4 parts grapefruit juice," how much juice will that recipe make? The answer is: any amount you want! This recipe uses a ratio that tells how things relate. The ratio of cranberry juice to grapefruit juice is 1 to 4. Ratios are often shown as fractions or decimals, such as $1/4$ or 0.25.

Let's say you are tossing a coin. On the first 10 coin tosses, the coin shows heads 6 times. On the next 10 tosses, it shows heads 4 times. After it is tossed 100 times, heads have shown 51 times. In this case the expected ratio of heads to tosses is 51 to 100. The theoretical, or ideal, ratio for tossing heads is 1 out of 2, $1/2$, or 0.50. An expected ratio tells what will probably happen after many throws. It can't predict the result of a single toss.

Is the ratio of boy births to all births the same as the heads-to-tosses ratio? Human history has shown there are 53 boys born for every 100 births. The expected ratio is 53 to 100. The expected ratio of males to all births among ants and bees is less than 1 to 100.

You can find a baseball player's batting average the same way you find the ratio of boy births to all births. Compare a player's hits for the season to his or her times at bat. If the player has 25 hits in 100 times at bat, the ratio, or batting average, is 0.250.

Batting averages can't determine what will happen the next time a player bats. However, if your team needs a hit, which one would you pick, a 0.300 hitter or a 0.100 hitter?

Discussion Starter

1 Using the recipe above, how much cranberry juice would you use to make 12 cups of fruit drink?

2 A nut mixture has a ratio of 1 almond for every 4 pecans. Is the ratio more like the ratio of juice to the whole drink or hits to at bats for a 0.250 batter? Why?

Predicting Traits

WHY IT MATTERS

Ratios can help determine how likely it is for some traits to be inherited.

What does it mean when a weather forecaster calls for a 50% chance of showers? Would you choose to carry an umbrella? Weather predictions are never absolutely certain.

What does predicting the weather have in common with genetics? What information would you need to gather if you wanted to predict the fur color of the offspring of two parent mice? As with the weather, you can never be really sure of your prediction.

SCIENCE WORDS

probability how likely it is for something to happen

Punnett square a table for predicting the outcome of crossing different forms of a trait

pedigree a chart used to trace the history of traits in a family

carrier an individual who has inherited a factor for a trait but does not show the trait

incomplete dominance a genetic pattern in which neither of the two forms of a trait completely masks the other

EXPLORE

HYPOTHESIZE How can you predict what traits offspring will have? Write a hypothesis in your *Science Journal*. How might you test your ideas?

Four factors control fur color in rabbits, but each rabbit inherits only two factors, one from each parent. The C factor is dominant over all the others, so any rabbit with at least one C factor has a gray coat. Other colors result from different combinations of the other three factors.

Multiple factors

WHY IT MATTERS

Understanding genetics has a lot to do with ratios and probability. Probability means that the results cannot be predicted, so scientists cannot be totally sure of what will happen. How does probability work in your life? What are your chances of getting to school on time? 50%? How can you increase the probability of getting to school on time so that you can be more sure of your result? You might get up earlier. You might pack your books the night before.

Brain Power

What else besides heredity might determine a person's body build and height?

REVIEW

1. What is a Punnett square used to show?

2. How are the factors different for a person with attached earlobes and a person with free earlobes?

3. USE NUMBERS Explain how it is possible for two parents, each with a dominant factor for dimples, to have a child without dimples. Draw a Punnett square to show your answer.

4. Dog breeders are very concerned about the pedigree of the dogs they raise and sell. What would a dog's pedigree tell you about the traits it expresses?

5. CRITICAL THINKING *Analyze* Can two white four-o'clocks produce a red four-o'clock offspring? Can two pink four-o'clocks produce red offspring?

WHY IT MATTERS THINK ABOUT IT
What is the probability of your school team winning an upcoming game? What can you do to be more sure that your team will do well?

WHY IT MATTERS WRITE ABOUT IT
How else is probability a part of your life? How can you increase the probability of getting the outcome that you want, rather than another outcome?

Pass It On

How do plants develop different characteristics from one generation to another? That's what many scientists wondered. In 1899 German botanist Karl Correns suggested that the characteristics are passed from generation to generation. Soon after, he discovered that a monk named Gregor Mendel had suggested that same theory 34 years earlier!

Strangely enough Hugo deVries of Holland came up with the same theory as Correns, at about the same time. Stranger still, another scientist showed deVries the paper Mendel had written in 1865!

What a dilemma! Correns and deVries planned to publish their theories that echoed Mendel's. Should they pretend they had never read the almost-unknown work or give the unknown monk credit? Both scientists did the right thing—they credited Mendel with the discovery.

Mendel was from a poor family. The only way he could get an education was to become a monk. After the monastery's gardener died, Mendel took over his duties and began to experiment with plant heredity.

For eight years Mendel grew peas and noted how the traits he'd selected were passed on from generation to generation. Finally he presented his research to the Natural Science Society in Austria.

The members of the society didn't exactly understand what Mendel said, but they published his work in their journal. His work didn't become well known because it covered genetics, about which little was known. Most other scientists rejected Mendel's findings.

Mendel's research was read by few until 1900 when Correns and deVries came to the same conclusion and were ethical enough to give him the credit he deserved.

Mendel (right) first presented the theory. More than 35 years later, deVries (left) and Correns came to the same conclusion.

Science, Technology, and Society

Once, this boy, who had ADA, a rare genetic disease that didn't let his body fight infection, had to live in a "bubble." Today such defective genes are replaced so kids with ADA can live normal lives.

DISCUSSION STARTER

1. When people need organ transplants, members of their families often have their genes "fingerprinted." Why?

2. If work, such as mining coal, is known to cause stress to genes, should job applicants have their genes tested? Should they be hired even if their genes might produce cancer?

To learn more about the genetics of disease, visit *www.mhschool.com/science* and select the keyword GENES.

SCIENCE WORDS

gene p.516

gene-splicing p.534

genetics p.485

heredity p.484

hybrid p.488

meiosis p.514

pedigree p.504

pollination p.486

probability p.498

Punnett square p.500

USING SCIENCE WORDS

Number a paper from 1 to 10. Fill in 1 to 5 with words from the list above.

1. A word for how likely it is that something will happen is ___?___.

2. The passing on of traits from parents to offspring is ___?___.

3. The result of crossing parents who have two different forms of the same trait is a(n) ___?___.

4. A table used to predict the outcome of a cross is a(n) ___?___.

5. The study of heredity is called ___?___.

6–10. Pick five words from the list above that were not used in 1 to 5, and use each in a sentence.

UNDERSTANDING SCIENCE IDEAS

11. What is the difference between selective breeding and genetic engineering?

12. What is the difference between self- and cross-pollination?

13. A purebred black dog is crossed with a purebred white dog. All the offspring have black-and-white fur. How can you explain this outcome?

14. What is meant by a sex-linked trait?

15. What are the four items used in the genetic code, and how are they grouped together?

USING IDEAS AND SKILLS

16. Describe how DNA is copied when a cell is ready to divide in two.

17. How does a cell with four chromosomes divide to form four sex cells?

18. **READING SKILL: SUMMARIZE** How did Mendel get a ratio of 3:1 when crossing tall pea plants?

19. **USE NUMBERS** Draw a Punnett square to show the probable outcomes of a cross between a woman who carries one sex-linked gene for hemophilia (X^hY) and a man who has no gene for hemophilia (XY).

20. **THINKING LIKE A SCIENTIST** What if the gene that causes sickle cell anemia has a slightly different arrangement of DNA base pairs than the gene for normal red blood cells? How might scientists go about developing a cure?

PROBLEMS and PUZZLES

Color Draw There are 5 buttons in a bag. You pick one out at a time and then put it back. When you do this 100 times, you pick

- a red button 18 times
  - a green button 44 times
    - a blue button 38 times

      How many red buttons are in the bag? Green buttons? Blue buttons?

Most of the fossils we find are left behind by organisms that no longer live on Earth. What happened to these organisms? Over time the environment on Earth has changed. We can tell environments changed by the changes shown in rocks, such as wearing away by wind or water. Areas may have been covered over with water. Areas that were once woodlands may have become grasslands.

As these changes took place, some species were not able to survive. When a species dies out because of changes in the environment, it becomes **extinct**. Examples of extinct organisms include the dinosaurs, the ancient animals you learned about in the Explore Activity, and the animals shown here.

As some species became extinct, other species developed. Fossils suggest that the newer species developed from changes in earlier species. The idea that species change over time, resulting in new species, is called the theory of **evolution**. This theory is supported by fossil evidence.

Most scientists believe that evolution explains how so many different forms of life have developed on Earth. According to this theory, Earth's environment determines which organisms survive. For example, the dinosaurs may have become extinct because of extreme changes in the environment. They were not able to survive the changes. As the dinosaurs died out, more food and space became available for mammals. Mammals began evolving much more rapidly than they had before.

The woolly mammoth and saber-toothed cat lived in North America almost two million years ago. The only evidence of their existence is the fossils they left behind.

What Kinds of Fossils Are There?

What lasts longer—a banana or a turtle's shell? An organism whose body has hard parts is more likely to become a fossil than a soft-bodied organism. Hooves, teeth, bones, shells, wood from a tree, and other hard parts are relatively slow to decay. They may not be eaten by other organisms. Hard parts are also not as easily broken. Traces of worms, jellyfish, leaves, flowers, and other soft plant and animal parts sometimes become fossils, but this rarely occurs.

Mineral Replacement

Mineral replacement is one way in which a fossil can form. Mineral-rich water can seep into bones, wood, or other hard material that is part of an organism's remains. The water dissolves the original material and replaces it with minerals. The minerals change the original material into stone. This kind of stone is much stronger and lasts much longer than the original organic material.

The mineralized fossil retains the same shape and reveals the details of the original material. In effect the

Petrified wood is an example of a mineralized fossil. Over millions of years, the wood in this log changed to stone.

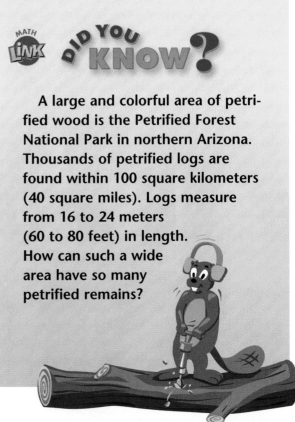

MATH LINK — DID YOU KNOW?

A large and colorful area of petrified wood is the Petrified Forest National Park in northern Arizona. Thousands of petrified logs are found within 100 square kilometers (40 square miles). Logs measure from 16 to 24 meters (60 to 80 feet) in length. How can such a wide area have so many petrified remains?

Learning about ancient forms of life makes people aware of how many forms of life have become extinct over time. Species today are still becoming extinct. Land developers are changing environments rapidly. Vast amounts of tropical rain forests are being destroyed. The Great Plains is being cemented over with highways and industrial parks. Species living in these areas are losing their habitats—and are dying out.

Cro-Magnon cave paintings from the Lascaux (läs kō′) **caves in France. The paintings occur deep inside the cave, so they were probably created by the light of crude torches or lamps.**

REVIEW

1. What conditions are necessary for the formation of fossils?

2. How is fossil formation by mineral replacement different from mold-and-cast fossil formation?

3. Besides fossils what other evidence is there that some forms of life have a common ancestor?

4. **COMPARE AND CONTRAST** What is the difference between relative age and absolute age?

5. **CRITICAL THINKING** *Apply* How does walking upright on two feet enable people to carry out their daily activities?

WHY IT MATTERS THINK ABOUT IT
What animals or plants have you heard of that are in danger of dying out, that is, are endangered? What is the cause?

WHY IT MATTERS WRITE ABOUT IT
Write a paragraph about why you chose the organism or object you would like to fossilize. Also write about how you would make your fossil. Share your ideas with classmates.

READING SKILL
Using the diagrams in this topic, describe how a fossil forms.

Whatever Became

Between 200 and 65 million years ago, dinosaurs were Earth's most common large land organisms. Then they vanished. Why? Only the dinosaurs know for sure, and they're not talking!

Some scientists say that global cooling caused the extinction. They believe the average global temperature 70 million years ago was about 20°C. By 65 million years ago, the average temperature was less than 15°C. Mammals and birds, protected by fur and feathers, fared better than dinosaurs during that time.

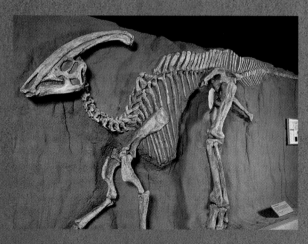

Duck-billed dinosaurs become extinct before 65 million years ago, posing a challenge to the impact theory.

In 1980 Walter and Luiz Alvarez found evidence that a giant asteroid had struck Earth 65 million years ago. Debris from the crash was found all around the world. The huge dust cloud sent up by such an impact, they say, would have blocked the Sun and caused global cooling and darkness.

Some people believe that Earth got hotter. They say the asteroid that hit Earth caused massive fires around the world. The carbon dioxide in the smoke trapped the Sun's energy and raised Earth's temperature.

Other people agree with the heat theory but believe it affected dinosaurs in a different way. They say that the

HUMAN BODY: RESPONSE AND CHANGE

CHAPTER 13

TWO SYSTEMS OF CONTROL

Do you tell your body what to do? How does it get the message? Do you always think about what you do before you do it? You don't have to tell your lungs to breathe or your heart to beat. They just do it. How?

Your body is a complex machine, so the more you know about it, the better you can keep it running. Why does your body act the way it does?

In this chapter summarize in a sentence or two what you read before you turn to a new page.

WHY IT MATTERS

The nervous system controls your ability to see, hear, smell, touch, and think.

SCIENCE WORDS

neuron an individual nerve cell

dendrite a nerve fiber that carries messages toward the cell body

axon a nerve fiber that carries messages away from the cell body

synapse the gap between neurons

sensory neuron a nerve cell that picks up stimuli and sends impulses produced by the stimuli to the brain and spinal cord

stimulus anything that causes a response

motor neuron a nerve cell that carries commands from the brain and spinal cord to the muscles and glands

associative neuron a nerve cell that passes impulses from sensory to motor neurons

The Nervous System

At lunchtime, how do you decide what to eat? How do you know that 2 + 2 = 4?

Your brain tells you. Your brain is the control center of your nervous system, which is made up of nerve cells. Nerve cells receive messages or signals and carry them from one part of your body to another. The brain, which itself is made of billions of nerve cells, interprets these messages and then sends messages to your body, causing it to act.

How does your nervous system work for you? How does your brain work so quickly?

EXPLORE

HYPOTHESIZE Your brain receives signals from different parts of your body, such as your nose, your ears, your fingertips. What signals do you respond most quickly to? Why? Write a hypothesis in your *Science Journal*. Test your ideas.

What's on Your Mind?

You sense things the way you do because of the ways in which your nerve cells are connected. Your brain is always busy finding out if your body parts are working right and making sure they stay that way. At the same time, it is receiving information about the world around you. It is deciding what you should do and where you should go. It controls your muscles, thoughts, and emotions. It allows you to remember the past and imagine the future. No machine invented yet can do so many things so quickly.

Take care of your nervous system. Wear protective gear when you play sports and do exercises. If you injure your brain or spinal cord, impulses won't be able to reach your muscles, and you won't be able to move. Stay away from drugs. Many drugs cause side effects like blurry vision and hearing loss. Stimulants, such as caffeine and nicotine, speed up the nervous system. They can cause the heart to overwork. Alcohol and other depressants slow down the nervous system.

REVIEW

1. How does the nervous system help us to protect ourselves?

2. What are the three kinds of neurons?

3. What are their functions?

4. **EXPERIMENT** Describe how you can test to see if your hands or your feet are more sensitive to touch.

5. **CRITICAL THINKING** *Evaluate* Is the central nervous system designed so that it can protect itself? How can you protect it further?

WHY IT MATTERS **THINK ABOUT IT**
Our nervous systems help us to protect ourselves. How does your nervous system help you in your daily life? What if you lived in the wilderness?

WHY IT MATTERS **WRITE ABOUT IT**
Imagine you lost the use of your sensory neurons. What would happen? What if you lost the use of your motor neurons? Your associative neurons?

A Nighttime MYSTERY

Researchers measure brain activity during sleep by attaching electrodes to a subject's head.

History of Science

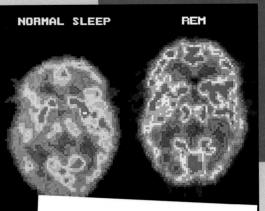

What happens in your brain when you're asleep? It's a mystery scientists are trying to solve. People sometimes think of sleep as the opposite of being awake, as if consciousness were either "on" or "off." We now know that sleep is a different state of consciousness, just as ice and vapor are two different states of water. What's more, sleep isn't one state, it's two. Researchers have found that sleepers drift back and forth between two kinds of sleep.

For thousands of years, no one knew this. People who were sleeping couldn't describe what happened when they slept. Then came the development of devices that could measure very small electric currents, such as those produced by the heart. In 1929 a German psychiatrist named Hans Berger connected the same kind of equipment to his son's skull. Berger detected electrical activity in the brain.

In 1952 Eugene Aserinsky used a later version of this machine, called an electroencephalograph (EEG) to measure the brain activity of sleeping people. He reported observing two types of sleep. During one type, even though the eyes are closed, the eyes of the sleeper move back and forth. Aserinsky named this type rapid-eye-movement (REM) sleep.

Each night a person experiences about 90 minutes of ordinary sleep, followed by 10 to 20 minutes of REM sleep. Then the pattern repeats. People awakened during REM sleep report vivid dreams. Since we all experience REM sleep, researchers believe that we all dream, even though some of us don't recall our dreams.

Brains scans show non-REM sleep (left) and REM sleep (right). Red areas are the most active; purple areas are least active.

Discussion Starter

1 Why were early researchers unable to learn about brain activity during sleep?

2 Cats often sleep for two-thirds of the day, while horses often sleep less than a quarter of the day. If the main function of sleep is to rest the muscles or the brain, what does this say about cats and horses?

*inter*NET CONNECTION To learn more about sleep and dreams, visit *www.mhschool.com/science* and enter the keyword **DREAM.**

WHY IT MATTERS

Your body uses chemicals to control many things.

SCIENCE WORDS

hormone a chemical that controls body functions by influencing how cells work

endocrine gland a gland that produces hormones

target organ the place in the body where a hormone acts

biological feedback the process the body uses to determine when to release a hormone and when to stop

metabolism the sum of all the chemical reactions that occur in your body

ovary the female reproductive organ, which produces eggs

testis the male reproductive organ, which produces sperm

The Endocrine System

Did you ever wonder how you grow? What controls your energy level? Your sleep? Your weight? Why does your body change as you become a teenager?

These changes are controlled by chemicals that travel in your bloodstream. Your body uses these chemicals to control how it works. Cells in one part of your body produce the chemicals and release them into your blood. Your blood carries the chemicals to their targets. Targets can be muscles, bones, or organs.

EXPLORE

HYPOTHESIZE Different organs in your body produce different chemicals. These chemicals cause changes in your body, but only when they reach their target. How can the blood carry chemicals to a target? Write a hypothesis in your *Science Journal*. Test your ideas.

Science, Technology, and Society

Sometimes, however, the only biochemical that works in humans is one made by humans. For example, an animal growth hormone can't be used to help a person who lacks sufficient human growth hormone (HGH).

By 1927 chemists were able to manufacture the active part of the thyroid hormone. It worked as well as the real hormone! Other hormones, like insulin and HGH, were too hard to copy. Chemist Russell Marker knew that plants make complex biochemicals with structures similar to many hormones. In the 1940s he used plants to make synthetic cortisone.

In the 1970s biologists learned to insert human genes into bacteria. One of the first successes was human insulin. By 1985 both human insulin and genetically engineered HGH were commercially available.

DISCUSSION STARTER

1. What four ways can hormones be obtained to treat people whose bodies don't produce enough?

2. Why might people whose diet is low in the iodine necessary for thyroid hormones develop an enlarged thyroid?

To learn more about hormones, visit *www.mhschool.com/science* and select the keyword HORMONES.

*inter*NET
CONNECTION

SCIENCE WORDS

biological feedback p.594	metabolism p.596
dendrite p.580	neuron p.580
endocrine gland p.594	ovary p.597
hormone p.594	stimulus p.581
	target organ p.594
	testis p.597

USING SCIENCE WORDS

Number a paper from 1 to 10. Fill in 1 to 5 with words from the list above.

1. A chemical that controls body functions by influencing how cells work is a(n) __?__.

2. The sum of all the chemical reactions in your body is called __?__.

3. The gap between neurons is a(n) __?__.

4. An individual nerve cell is a(n) __?__.

5. The place in the body where a hormone acts is a(n) __?__.

6–10. **Pick five words from the list above that were not used in 1 to 5, and use each in a sentence.**

UNDERSTANDING SCIENCE IDEAS

11. As a living cell, how does a neuron receive nutrients and dispose of waste? What else does a neuron need to function?

12. Describe a situation in which the spinal cord protects you from danger.

13. What makes the pancreas different from other endocrine glands?

14. How can too much or too little of a hormone cause health problems? Give two examples.

15. How do receptors work to make cells respond to certain stimuli? How do they work in target organs?

USING IDEAS AND SKILLS

16. **EXPERIMENT** How does the amount of light affect the colors you see? How would you set up an experiment to investigate this question?

17. **READING SKILL: SUMMARIZE** How can drugs affect a person's nervous system? Why is it dangerous to drink alcohol and then drive a car?

18. A person with diabetes must check the amount of sugar he gets in his diet. Why is sugar intake so important to him?

19. Draw a diagram, and describe how an impulse travels through a nerve cell, including in your description the dendrites, axon, and synapse.

20. **THINKING LIKE A SCIENTIST** Why is it necessary for hormones to have longer-lasting effects than nerve impulses?

PROBLEMS and PUZZLES

Hole in One Roll up a piece of paper into a tube. Look through the tube at an object in the distance. Now hold your free hand up against the tube, palm facing you. Look with both eyes. What happens to your free hand? Why do your eyes create this optical illusion?

Skills: Making a Model and Communicating

ART LINK

HOW TWINS FORM

Twins can be identical. That is, they form from a single zygote that splits in two. They look alike and are the same sex. Twins can be fraternal. They form from two separate eggs that are fertilized separately.

You can make a model to show how twins can be identical or fraternal. Models are also useful to communicate ideas with others. Compare your models with those that others made to see how any one model can be most accurate.

MATERIALS

- clay in various colors or other art materials
- *Science Journal*

PROCEDURES

1. MAKE A MODEL You will make small balls of clay to represent cells. You can choose different colors to represent sperm and egg cells. You may also use different colors to show that some twins can be male and some female.

2. PLAN Decide how you will represent the way identical twins form and the way fraternal twins form. Record your ideas in your *Science Journal*. Show as many combinations of fraternal twins as you can.

3. COMMUNICATE Present your models to others. Ask if they can tell the difference between the models for identical twins and fraternal twins.

CONCLUDE AND APPLY

1. EVALUATE How well did your model show why some twins are identical and others are fraternal? What might you do to make your model clearer?

2. INFER How might you show the way identical triplets or quadruplets are formed?

Identical twins developed from one zygote.

Is the Baby Ready to Be Born?

What happens when a baby is born? First, hormones from the mother's pituitary gland target the muscles of her uterus. The muscles begin to contract and relax, first gently, then more strongly. The contractions may last for hours and cause the mother labor pain. The sac of fluids around the baby breaks as the uterus's muscles start to push the baby out of the uterus and into the vagina. Together the uterus and vagina become the birth canal.

The bones in the baby's skull are so soft that the head can change shape as it passes through the birth canal. The contractions continue to push the baby along. Finally, the baby's head and shoulders emerge from the mother's body. With a few more contractions, the baby is completely born, with the umbilical cord still attached.

Immediately the baby is held upside down to remove swallowed fluids from the lungs. Then the baby takes its first breath of air. Because the baby can now survive without oxygen from the mother's blood, the umbilical cord is cut. The cord has no nerves in it, so the baby feels no pain. However, a small piece of the cord is left on the baby's body. It becomes what you know as a navel, or bellybutton.

Brain Power

Porpoises carry their babies in a uterus as humans do. The baby is born tail first though. Can you explain why?

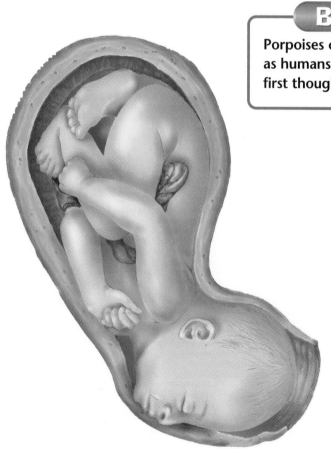

The contractions of the muscles in the uterus push the baby out of its mother's body.

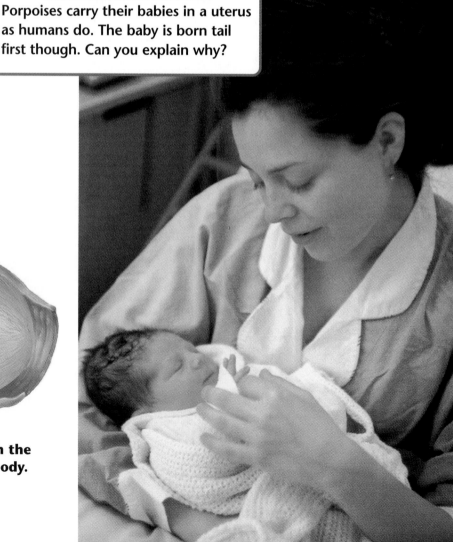

What Is a Sexually Transmitted Disease?

The job of the reproductive system is to produce a new life. That involves direct contact between body parts and the exchange of body fluids. Because of this contact, diseases called sexually transmitted diseases, or STDs, may be spread. These include syphilis, gonorrhea, and genital herpes. Many STDs can be deadly if untreated.

The only sure, effective way to avoid these diseases is abstinence. To *abstain* means to "choose not to do something." Abstinence is choosing not to be sexually active.

STDs can be frightening. Turn to your family for support and information.

The body becomes ready for reproduction as a person reaches puberty. However, a young person still has to grow in many ways before being ready to become a parent. Learning how to support a family, how to develop thinking skills and interests, how to relate with others—these are just a few of the ways a person must grow along the way to being an effective parent.

REVIEW

1. Where are sex cells produced in the human body?

2. Where does fertilization occur? What happens after it occurs?

3. How does the developing baby get food and oxygen? Protection?

4. **MAKE A MODEL/COMMUNICATE** How could you make a model to show a difference between female identical twins and female fraternal twins?

5. **CRITICAL THINKING** *Synthesize* How does reproduction ensure the survival of a species?

WHY IT MATTERS THINK ABOUT IT
What changes do you observe taking place in your body? How is your body preparing itself to reproduce?

WHY IT MATTERS WRITE ABOUT IT
Does the ability to have offspring indicate the ability to take care of offspring? Why or why not?

READING SKILL
What are some details that support the main idea that a new baby develops inside the uterus?

Making a New Life

Nature has many ways to keep Earth populated. Fish make new life through external fertilization. A female lays eggs on a plant or rock underwater, then the male sprays them with semen.

Animals that reproduce by external fertilization have organs to produce egg and sperm cells, but they don't need or have a penis, vagina, or placenta.

External fertilization works only in water, because it provides the wet environment sperm need to survive. Animals that live on land reproduce through internal fertilization.

During internal fertilization, a male's penis deposits semen inside the female's vagina. In that moist environment, the sperm live long enough to fertilize the eggs.

The male spider doesn't have a penis but still uses internal fertilization. The male wraps his sperm in the silk he uses to spin a web, then puts the package inside the female's body.

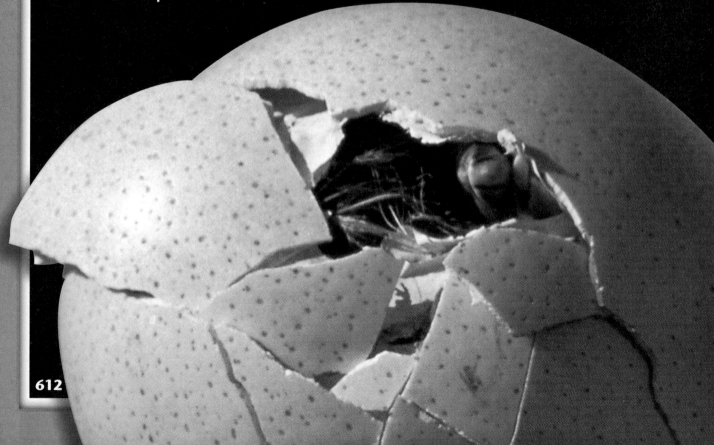

REFERENCE SECTION

DIAGRAM BUILDERS

Building a Topographic Map

A topographic map uses **contour lines** to show the shape of the land. A contour line is drawn through points of a given height, or elevation, above or below sea level. **How do contour lines show the shape of the land?**

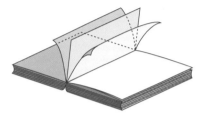

BASE

To find out, look at the map on the facing page. Lift up all the plastic overlays (1, 2, 3), and look at the base. You see an area of land as if you were looking down from an airplane.
Do you see the landforms?

OVERLAY 1

1 Now drop overlay 1 onto the base. From one contour line to the next is a difference of 1,000 meters in elevation. That difference is not a measure of how far apart the lines are. To tell that, measure the distance between any two lines and compare the distance to the map scale.
Do the contour lines help you see any landforms or the shape of the land? How?

OVERLAY 2

2 Now drop overlay 2 onto overlay 1. The contour lines are now drawn for every 500 meters.
Can you see the shape of the land better than with just overlay 1? Explain.

OVERLAY 3

3 Now drop overlay 3 onto overlay 2.
What details are added? How do they complete the picture?

SUMMARIZE

How do the lines of a contour map help you tell which places are steeper than others?

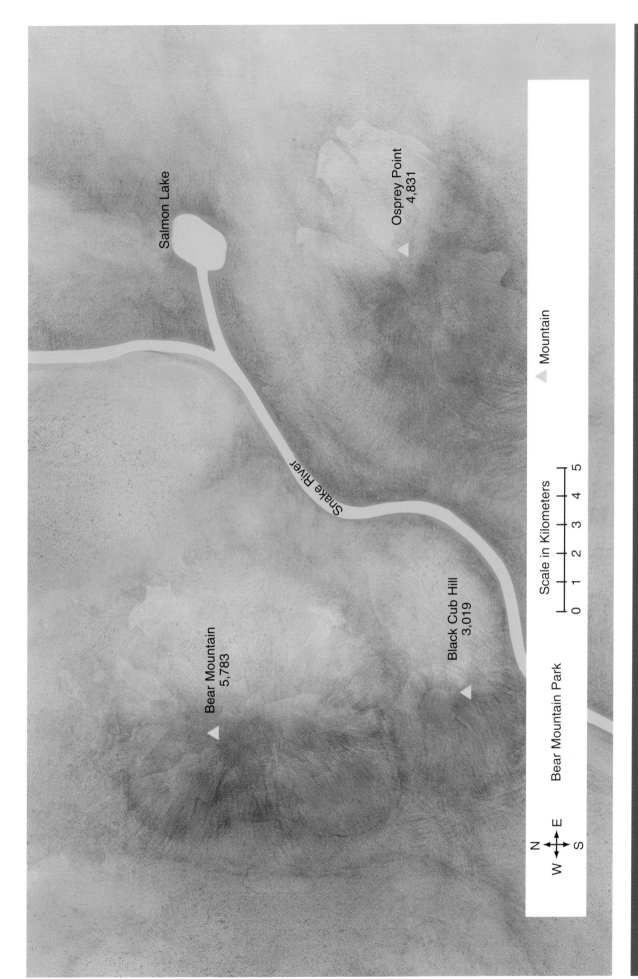

N
W + E
S

▲ Mountain

Bear Mountain Park

Scale in Kilometers

0 1 2 3 4 5

Salmon Lake

Snake River

Bear Mountain
5,783

Black Cub Hill
3,019

Osprey Point
4,831

BASE: Start with Bear Mountain Park.

DIAGRAM BUILDERS
Activities

1 Make a Map

You need: compass, graph paper, meterstick or tape measure

Make a map of a room, your school playground, or any small area. Use the compass to tell what the direction of each corner is. Measure the sides. Decide how many squares of a graph paper grid you would need to show the area. What real length would each side of a graph paper square represent?

2 Make Observations

You need: washers, string, ruler

Hang a heavy weight, like a bunch of washers, on a string to make what is called a plumb line. Tie the free end of the string to the end of a ruler. Hold the free end of the ruler down onto your shoulder so that the string and weight are hanging alongside your body. How can you use this string and weight to tell if you are walking along a level surface or you are going up or down a slanted surface? Explain.

3 Write About a Main Idea

How can a contour map help you study changes in an area? Think of an area, for example, along a shoreline that is hit by strong waves or an area that has frequent earthquakes.

REFERENCE SECTION

HANDBOOK

This bottle of juice has a volume of 1 liter.

That is a little more than 1 quart.

She can walk 20 meters in 5 seconds.

That means her speed is 4 meters per second.

Table of Measurements

SI (INTERNATIONAL SYSTEM) OF UNITS

Temperature

Water freezes at 0°C and boils at 100°C.

Length and Distance

1,000 meters = 1 kilometer
100 centimeters = 1 meter
10 millimeters = 1 centimeter

Volume

1,000 milliliters = 1 liter
1 cubic centimeter = 1 milliliter

Mass

1,000 grams = 1 kilogram

ENGLISH SYSTEM OF UNITS

Temperature

Water freezes at 32°F and boils at 212°F.

Length and Distance

5,280 feet = 1 mile
3 feet = 1 yard
12 inches = 1 foot

Volume of Fluids

4 quarts = 1 gallon
2 pints = 1 quart
2 cups = 1 pint
8 fluid ounces = 1 cup

Weight

2,000 pounds = 1 ton
16 ounces = 1 pound

In the Classroom

The most important part of doing any experiment is doing it safely. You can be safe by paying attention to your teacher and doing your work carefully. Here are some other ways to stay safe while you do experiments.

Before the Experiment

- Read all of the directions. Make sure you understand them. When you see be sure to follow the safety rule.

- Listen to your teacher for special safety directions. If you don't understand something, ask for help.
- Wash your hands with soap and water before an activity.

During the Experiment

- Wear safety goggles when your teacher tells you to wear them and whenever you see .
- Wear splash-proof goggles when working with liquids.
- Wear goggles when working with anything that can fly into your eyes.
- Wear a safety apron if you work with anything messy or anything that might spill.
- If you spill something, wipe it up right away or ask your teacher for help.

- Tell your teacher if something breaks. If glass breaks do not clean it up yourself.
- Keep your hair and clothes away from open flames. Tie back long hair and roll up long sleeves.
- Be careful around a hot plate. Know when it is on and when it is off. Remember that the plate stays hot for a few minutes after you turn it off.
- Keep your hands dry around electrical equipment.
- Don't eat or drink anything during the experiment.

After the Experiment

- Put equipment back the way your teacher tells you.
- Dispose of things the way your teacher tells you.
- Clean up your work area and wash your hands with soap and water.

In the Field

- Always be accompanied by a trusted adult—like your teacher or a parent or guardian.
- Never touch animals or plants without the adult's approval. The animal might bite. The plant might be poison ivy or another dangerous plant.

Responsibility

Acting safely is one way to be responsible. You can also be responsible by treating animals, the environment, and each other with respect in the class and in the field.

Treat Living Things with Respect

- If you have animals in the classroom, keep their homes clean. Change the water in fish tanks and clean out cages.
- Feed classroom animals the right amount of food.
- Give your classroom animals enough space.
- When you observe animals, don't hurt them or disturb their homes.
- Find a way to care for animals while school is on vacation.

Treat the Environment with Respect

- Do not pick flowers.
- Do not litter, including gum and food.
- If you see litter, ask your teacher if you can pick it up.
- Recycle materials used in experiments. Ask your teacher what materials can be recycled instead of thrown away. These might include plastics, aluminum, and newspapers.

Treat Each Other with Respect

- Use materials carefully around others so that people don't get hurt or get stains on their clothes.
- Be careful not to bump people when they are doing experiments. Do not disturb or damage their experiments.
- If you see that people are having trouble with an experiment, help them.

Use a Hand Lens

One of the most important things you do in science is something that you do every day—make observations. You make an observation every time you use your senses to learn about the world around you. Whether you are watching a bird build a nest, listening to the rumble of distant thunder, or feeling the pull of a refrigerator magnet, you are using your senses to learn.

Sometimes your senses need a little help, especially during experiments. A hand lens, for example, magnifies an object, or makes the object look larger. With a hand lens, you can see details that would be hard to see otherwise.

Magnify a Piece of Cereal

1. Place a piece of your favorite cereal on a flat surface. Look at the cereal carefully. Draw a picture of it.
2. Look at the cereal through the large lens of a hand lens. Move the lens toward or away from the cereal until it looks larger and in focus. Draw a picture of the cereal as you see it through the hand lens. Fill in details that you did not see before.
3. Look at the cereal through the smaller lens, which will magnify the cereal even more. If you notice more details, add them to your drawing.
4. Repeat this activity using objects you are studying in science. It might be a rock, some soil, or a seed.

Observe Mold in a Petri Dish

A petri dish is a shallow, clear, round dish with a cover. It's useful for growing microscopic organisms such as mold.

1. Place a piece of bread about the size of your palm in a petri dish. It is best if the bread is a few days old and not made with preservatives.
2. Wet the bread by sprinkling water on it. Put the lid on the petri dish, and place the dish in a warm place.
3. After a few days, mold will start to grow on the bread. Use a hand lens to observe the mold through the clear petri dish. Draw what you see. Do not remove the cover from the dish.

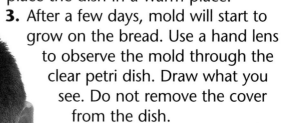

Temperature

You use a thermometer to measure temperature—how hot or cold something is. A thermometer is made of a thin tube with colored liquid inside. When the liquid gets warmer, it expands and moves up the tube. When the liquid gets cooler, it contracts and moves down the tube. You may have seen most temperatures measured in degrees Fahrenheit (°F). Scientists measure temperature in degrees Celsius (°C).

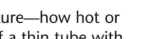

Read a Thermometer

1. Look at the thermometer shown here. It has two scales—a Fahrenheit scale and a Celsius scale. Every 20 degrees on the Fahrenheit scale has a number. Every 10 degrees on the Celsius scale has a number.
2. What is the temperature shown on the thermometer? At what temperature does water freeze? Give your answers in °F and in °C.

What Is Convection?

1. Fill a large beaker about two-thirds full of cool water. Find the temperature of the water by holding a thermometer in the water. Do not let the bulb at the bottom of the thermometer touch the sides or bottom of the beaker.
2. Keep the thermometer in the water until the liquid in the tube stops moving—about a minute. Read and record the temperature in °C.

3. Sprinkle a little fish food on the surface of the water in the beaker. Do not knock the beaker, and most of the food will stay on top.
4. Carefully place the beaker on a hot plate. A hot plate is a small electric stove. Plug in the hot plate, and turn the control knob to a middle setting.
5. After a minute measure the temperature of water near the bottom of the beaker. At the same time, a classmate should measure the temperature of water near the top of the beaker. Record these temperatures. Is water near the bottom of the beaker heating up faster than near the top?
6. As the water heats up, notice what happens to the fish food. How do you know that warmer water at the bottom of the beaker rises and cooler water at the top sinks?

Weather

What information is included in a weather report? You might think of temperature, cloud cover, wind speed, amount of rainfall, and so on. Various instruments are used to measure these parts of the weather. Some of them are shown here.

Barometer

A barometer measures air pressure. Most barometers are like the one shown here. It contains a flat metal can with most of the air removed. When air pressure increases (rises), the air pushes more on the can. A pointer that is attached to the can moves toward a higher number on the scale. When air pressure decreases (falls), the air pushes less on the can. The pointer moves toward a lower number on the scale.

29.73 inches ⟶

Notice that the barometer above measures air pressure in inches and in centimeters. The long arrow points to the current air pressure, which is 29.73 inches of mercury. That means the air pushing down on liquid mercury in a dish would force the mercury 29.73 inches up a tube, as the drawing shows. What is the air pressure in centimeters?

Follow these steps when you use a barometer.

1. Look at the current air pressure reading marked by the long arrow.
2. Turn the knob on the front of the barometer so the short arrow points to the current pressure reading.
3. Check the barometer several times a day to see if the pressure is rising, falling, or staying the same.

Rain Gauge

A rain gauge measures how much rain falls. This instrument is simply a container that collects water. It has one or more scales for measuring the amount of rain.

The rain gauge shown here has been collecting rain throughout the day. How much rain fell in inches? In centimeters?

Weather Vane

A weather vane measures wind direction. A weather vane is basically an arrow that is free to spin on a pole. Wind pushes on the widest part of the arrow—the tail—so that the arrow points to the direction that the wind is coming from. Letters on the weather vane show directions. If the vane doesn't have letters, you can tell direction with a compass. What direction is the wind coming from in the picture?

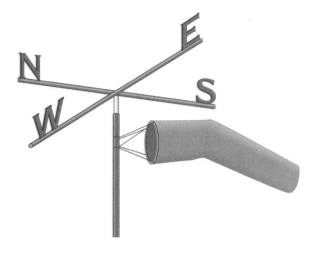

Windsock

A windsock also measures wind direction. You may have seen windsocks at airports. Windsocks are usually large and bright orange so that pilots can easily see which way the wind is blowing. The large opening of the windsock faces the wind. The narrow part of the windsock points in the direction that the wind is blowing. Which way is the wind blowing in the picture?

Anemometer

An anemometer measures wind speed. It is usually made of three shallow cones, or cups, that spin on an axle. The wind makes the cups and axle spin. The axle is attached to a dial that indicates wind speed. The faster the wind blows, the faster the cups turn.

Computer

A computer has many uses. The Internet connects your computer to many other computers around the world, so you can collect all kinds of information. You can use a computer to show this information and write reports. Best of all you can use a computer to explore, discover, and learn.

You can also get information from CD-ROMs. They are computer disks that can hold large amounts of information. You can fit a whole encyclopedia on one CD-ROM.

Use Computers for a Project

Here is how one group of students uses computers as they work on a weather project.

1. The students use instruments to measure temperature, wind speed, wind direction, and other parts of the weather. They input this information, or data, into the computer. The students keep the data in a table. This helps them compare the data from one day to the next.

2. The teacher finds out that another group of students in a town 200 kilometers to the west is also doing a weather project. The two groups use the Internet to talk to each other and share data. When a storm happens in the town to the west, that group tells the other group that it's coming its way.

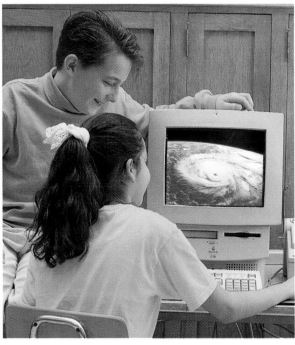

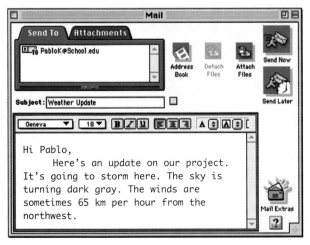

3. The students want to find out more. They decide to stay on the Internet and send questions to a local TV weather forecaster. She has a Web site and answers questions from students every day.

4. Meanwhile some students go to the library to gather more information from a CD-ROM disk. The CD-ROM has an encyclopedia that includes movie clips with sound. The clips give examples of different kinds of storms.

5. The students have kept all their information in a folder called Weather Project. Now they use that information to write a report about the weather. On the computer they can move around paragraphs, add words, take out words, put in diagrams, and draw their own weather maps. Then they print the report in color.

Calculator

Sometimes after you make measurements, you have to analyze your data to see what it means. This might involve doing calculations with your data. A calculator helps you do time-consuming calculations.

Find an Average

After you collect a set of measurements, you may want to get an idea of a typical measurement in that set. What if, for example, you are doing a weather project? As part of the project, you are studying rainfall data of a nearby town. The table shows how much rain fell in that town each week during the summer.

Week	Rain (cm)
1	2.0
2	1.4
3	0.0
4	0.5
5	1.2
6	2.5
7	1.8
8	1.4
9	2.4
10	8.6
11	7.5

What if you want to get an idea of how much rain fell during a typical week in the summer? In other words you want to find the average for the set of data. There are three kinds of averages— mean, median, and mode. Does it matter which one you use?

Find the Mean

The mean is what most people think of when they hear the word *average*. You can use a calculator to find the mean.

1. Make sure the calculator is on.
2. Add the numbers. To add a series of numbers, enter the first number and press ⊞. Repeat until you enter the last number. See the hints below. After your last number, press ⊟. Your total should be 29.3.
3. While entering so many numbers, it's easy to make a mistake and hit the wrong key. If you make a mistake, correct it by pressing the clear entry key, **CE**. Then continue entering the rest of the numbers.
4. Find the mean by dividing your total by the number of weeks. If 29.3 is displayed, press ⊡ ① ① ⊟. Rounded up to one decimal point, your mean should be 2.7.

Hints:

- If the only number to the right of the decimal point is 0, you don't have to enter it into the calculator. To enter 2.0, just press ②.
- If the only number to the left of the decimal point is 0, you don't have to enter it into the calculator. To enter 0.5, just press ⦁ ⑤.

Find the Median

The median is the middle number when the numbers are arranged in order of size. When the rainfall measurements are arranged in order of size, they look like this.

0.0
0.5
1.2   The median is
1.4   1.8. This number
1.4   is in the middle;
1.8 ←—there are five
2.0   numbers above
2.4   it and five
2.5   numbers below it.
7.5
8.6

Find the Mode

The mode is the number that occurs most frequently. From the ranked set of data above, you can see that the most frequent number is 1.4. It occurs twice. Here are your three different averages from the same set of data.

Average Weekly Rainfall (cm)

Mean	**2.7**
Median	**1.8**
Mode	**1.4**

Why is the mean so much higher than the median or mode? The mean is affected greatly by the last two weeks when it rained a lot. A typical week for that summer was much drier than either of those last two weeks. The median or mode gives a better idea of rainfall for a typical week.

Find the Mean, Median, and Mode

The table shows the length of 15 peanuts. Find the mean, median, and mode for this set of data. Which do you think best represents a typical peanut?

Peanut	Length (mm)
1	32
2	29
3	30
4	31
5	33
6	26
7	28
8	27
9	29
10	29
11	32
12	31
13	23
14	36
15	31

Find the Percent

Sometimes numbers are given as percents (%). *Percent* literally means "per hundred." For example, 28% means 28 out of 100. What if there are about 14,000 trees in the forest and 28% are over 50 years old? How many of them are over 50 years old? Use your calculator. You want to find 28% of 14,000. Press 1 4 0 0 0 × 2 8 %. The answer should be 3,920.

Make Graphs to Organize Data

When you do an experiment in science, you collect information. To find out what your information means, you can organize it into graphs. There are many kinds of graphs.

Circle Graphs

A circle graph is helpful to show how a complete set of data is divided into parts. The circle graph here shows how water is used in the United States. What is the single largest use of water?

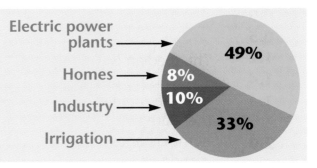

Electric power plants → 49%
Homes → 8%
Industry → 10%
Irrigation → 33%

Bar Graphs

A bar graph uses bars to show information. For example, what if you wrap wire around a nail and connect the ends to a battery? The nail becomes a magnet that can pick up paper clips. The graph shows that the more you wrap the wire around the nail, the more paper clips it picks up.

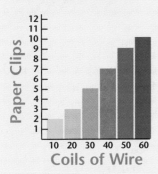

How many paper clips did the nail with 20 coils pick up? With 50 coils?

Line Graphs

A line graph shows information by connecting dots plotted on the graph. For example, what if you are growing a plant? Every week you measure how high the plant has grown. The line graph below organizes the measurements.

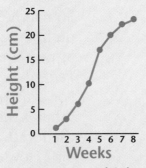

1. Between which two weeks did the plant grow most?
2. When did plant growth begin to level off?

Make a Graph

What if you collect information about how much water your family uses each day?

Activity	Water Used (L)
Drinking	10
Showering	180
Bathing	240
Brushing teeth	80
Washing dishes	140
Washing hands	30
Washing clothes	280
Flushing toilet	90

Decide what type of graph would best organize such data. Collect the information, and make your graph. Compare it with those of classmates.

Make Maps to Show Information

Locate Places

A map is a drawing that shows an area from above. Most maps have coordinates—numbers and letters along the top and side. Coordinates help you find places easily. For example, what if you wanted to find the library on the map? It is located at B4. Place a finger on the letter B at the top of the map and another finger on the number 4 along the side. Then move your fingers straight across and down the map until they meet. The library is located where the coordinates B and 4 meet, or very nearby.

1. What color building is located at F6?
2. The hospital is located three blocks north and two blocks east of the library. What are its coordinates?
3. Make a map of an area in your community. It might be a park or the area between your home and school. Include coordinates. Use a compass to find north, and mark north on your map. Exchange maps with classmates, and answer each other's questions.

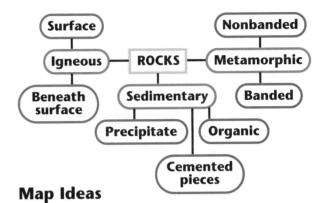

Map Ideas

The map shows how places are connected to each other. Idea maps, on the other hand, show how ideas are connected to each other. Idea maps help you organize information about a topic.

The idea map above connects ideas about rocks. This map shows that there are three major types of rock—igneous, sedimentary, and metamorphic. Connections to each rock type provide further information. For example, this map reminds you that igneous rocks are classified into those that form at Earth's surface and far beneath it.

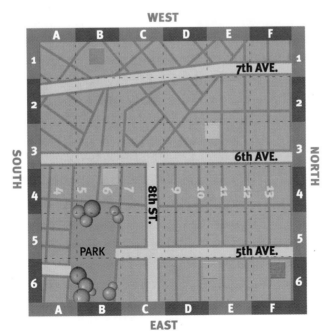

Make an idea map about a topic you are learning in science. Your map can include words, phrases, or even sentences. Arrange your map in a way that makes sense to you and helps you understand the ideas.

Make Tables and Charts to Organize Information

Tables help you organize data during experiments. Most tables have columns that run up and down, and rows that run across. The columns and rows have headings that tell you what kind of data goes in each part of the table.

A Sample Table

What if you are going to do an experiment to find out how long different kinds of seeds take to sprout? Before you begin the experiment, you should set up your table. Follow these steps.

1. In this experiment you will plant 20 radish seeds, 20 bean seeds, and 20 corn seeds. Your table must show how many radish seeds, bean seeds, and corn seeds sprouted on days 1, 2, 3, 4, and 5.

2. Make your table with columns, rows, and headings. You might use a computer to make a table. Some computer programs let you build a table with just the click of a mouse. You can delete or add columns and rows if you need to.

3. Give your table a title. Your table could look like the one here.

Make a Table

Now what if you are going to do an experiment to find out how temperature affects the sprouting of seeds? You will plant 20 bean seeds in each of two trays. You will keep each tray at a different temperature, as shown below, and observe the trays for seven days. Make a table you can use for this experiment.

Make a Chart

A chart is simply a table with pictures as well as words to label the rows or columns.

HANDBOOK

INDEX

*Indicates an activity related to this topic.

INDEX

*Indicates an activity related to this topic.

PERIODIC TABLE OF THE ELEMENTS

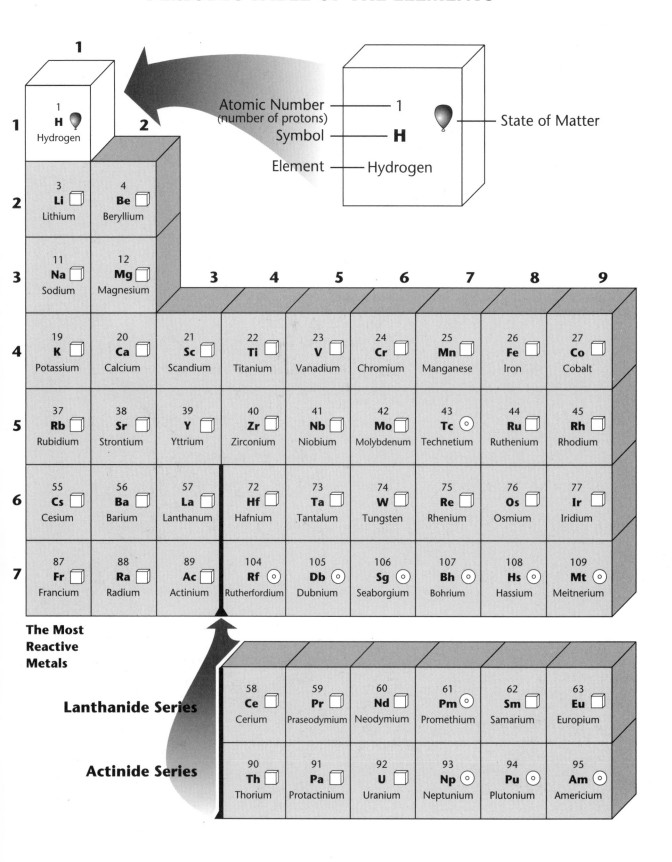